VALEAS MUNDUM

ANDY RILEY HAS WRITTEN FOR BLACK BOOKS, TRIGGER HAPPY TV, SO GRAHAM NORTON AND SMACK THE PONY. HE HAS CO-WRITTEN THE BAFTA AWARD-WINNING ROBBIE THE REINDEER, THE RADIO FOUR PANEL GAME THE 99p CHALLENGE AND A DISNEY ANIMATION FEATURE, GNOMEO AND JULIET, TO BE RELEASED IN 2005. HE ALSO HAS A WEEKLY COMIC STRIP IN THE OBSERVER MAGAZINE.

THE BOOK OF
BUNNY SUICIDES

ANDY RILEY

A PLUME BOOK

PLUME

PUBLISHED BY THE PENGUIN GROUP

PENGUIN GROUP (USA) INC., 375 HUDSON STREET, NEW YORK, NEW YORK 10014, USA
PENGUIN BOOKS LTD, 80 STRAND, LONDON WC2R ORL, ENGLAND
PENGUIN BOOKS AUSTRALIA LTD, 250 CAMBERWELL ROAD, CAMBERWELL, VICTORIA 3124, AUSTRALIA
PENGUIN BOOKS CANADA LTD, 10 ALCORN AVENUE, TORONTO, ONTARIO, CANADA M4V 3B2
PENGUIN BOOKS INDIA (P) LTD, 11 COMMUNITY CENTRE, PANCHSHEEL PARK, NEW DELHI - 110 017, INDIA
PENGUIN BOOKS (NZ) LTD, CNR ROSEDALE AND AIRBORNE ROADS, ALBANY, AUCKLAND 1310, NEW ZEALAND
PENGUIN BOOKS (SOUTH AFRICA) (PTY) LTD, 24 STURDEE AVENUE, ROSEBANK, JOHANNESBURG 2196, SOUTH AFRICA

PENGUIN BOOKS LTD, REGISTERED OFFICES: 80 STRAND, LONDON WC2R ORL, ENGLAND

PUBLISHED BY PLUME, A MEMBER OF THE PENGUIN GROUP (USA) INC. THIS IS AN AUTHORIZED REPRINT OF A HARDCOVER EDITION PUBLISHED BY HODDER & STOUGHTON, 338 EUSTON ROAD, LONDON NW1 3BH, ENGLAND

FIRST PLUME PRINTING, JANUARY 2004
10 9 8 7 6 5 4

CIP DATA IS AVAILABLE. ISBN 0-452-28518-6

NC1479.R55A4 2003
741.5'973 - dc22 2003060366

PRINTED IN THE UNITED STATES OF AMERICA

WITH THANKS TO

KEVIN CECIL, ARTHUR MATHEWS

AND ALSO...

POLLY FABER, CAMILLA HORNBY,
KATY FOLLAIN + AMANDA SCHOENWALD

FOR POLLY

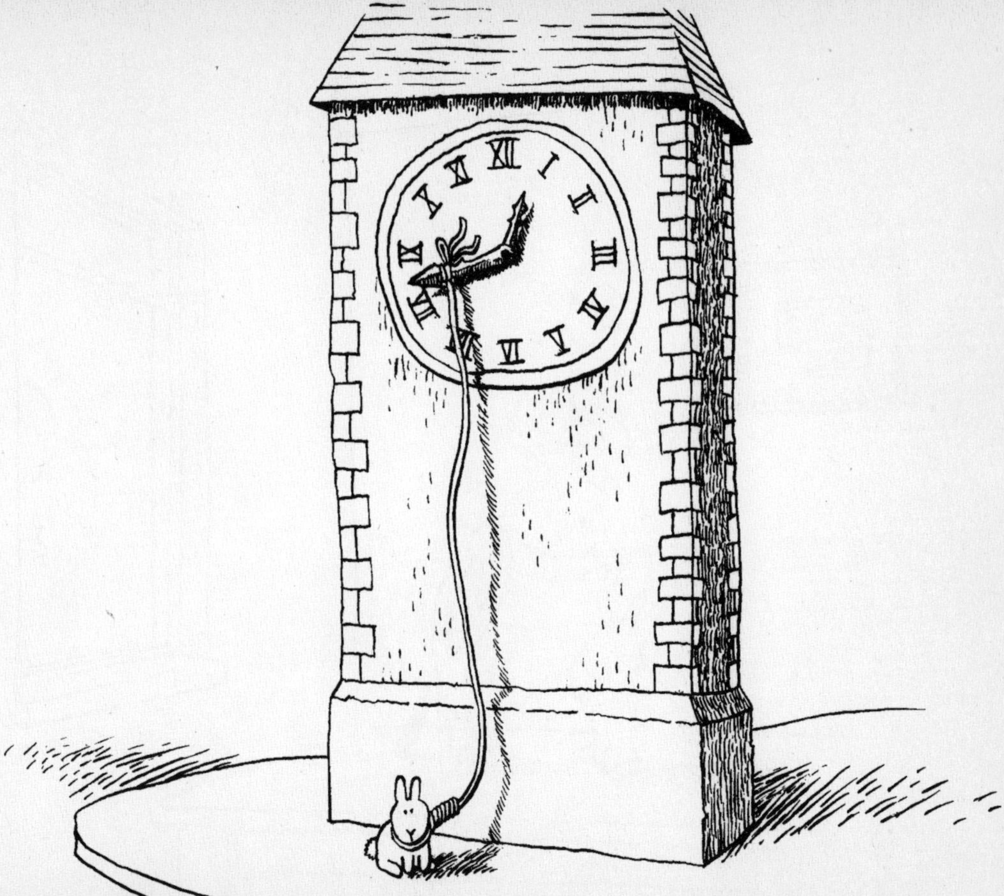

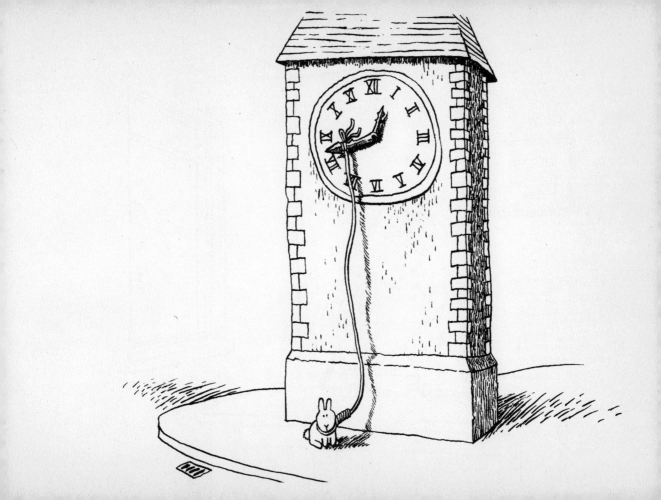

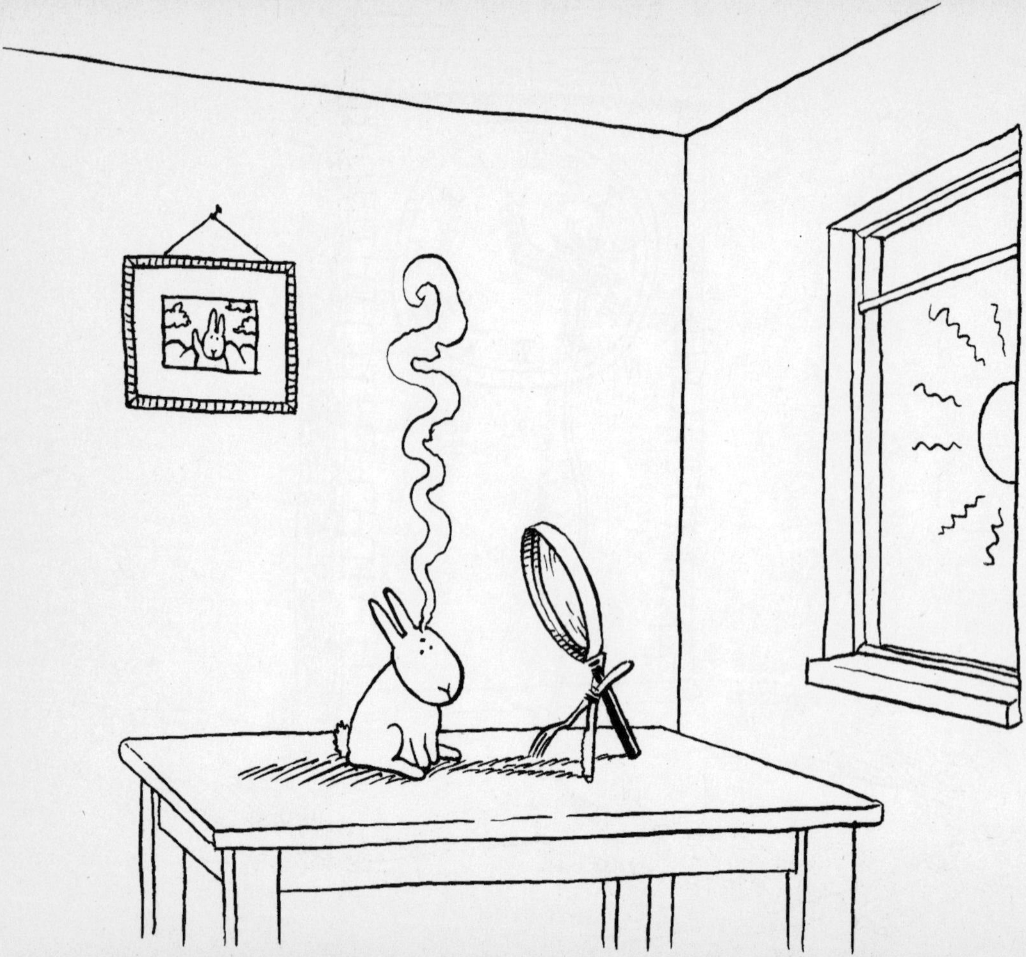

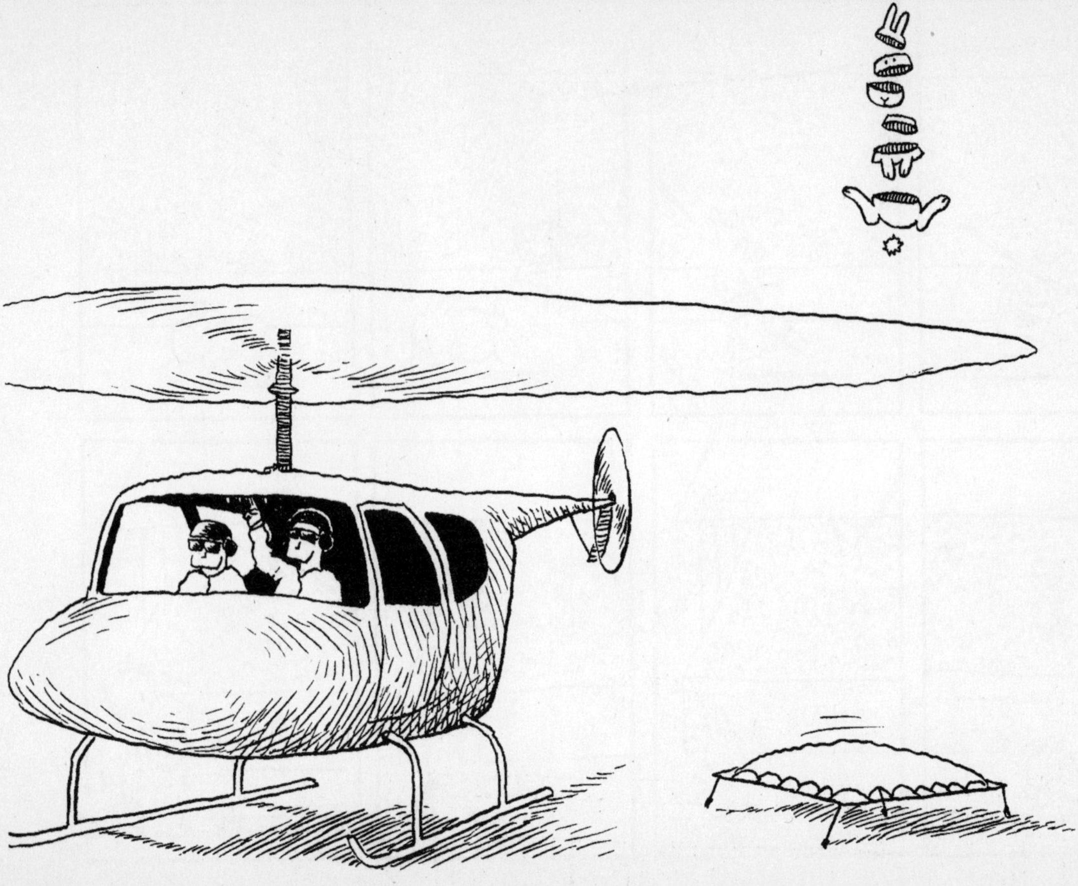

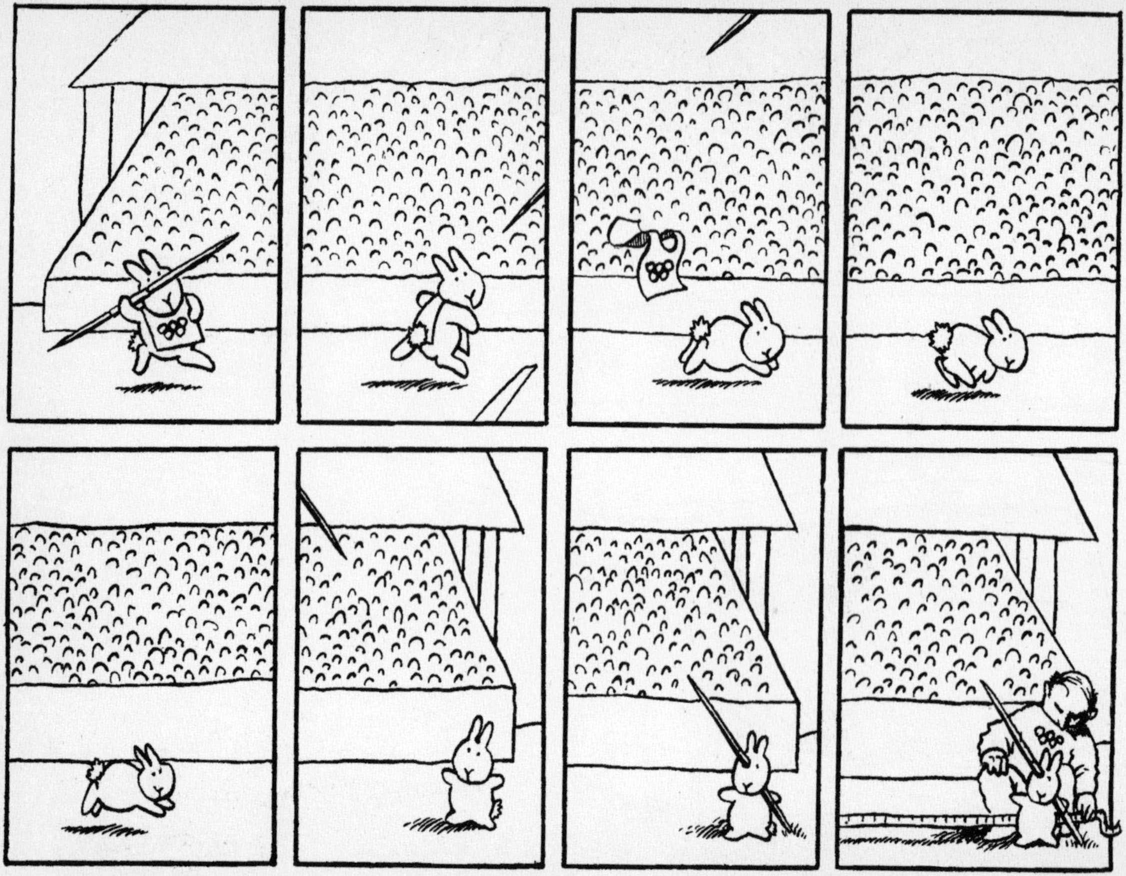

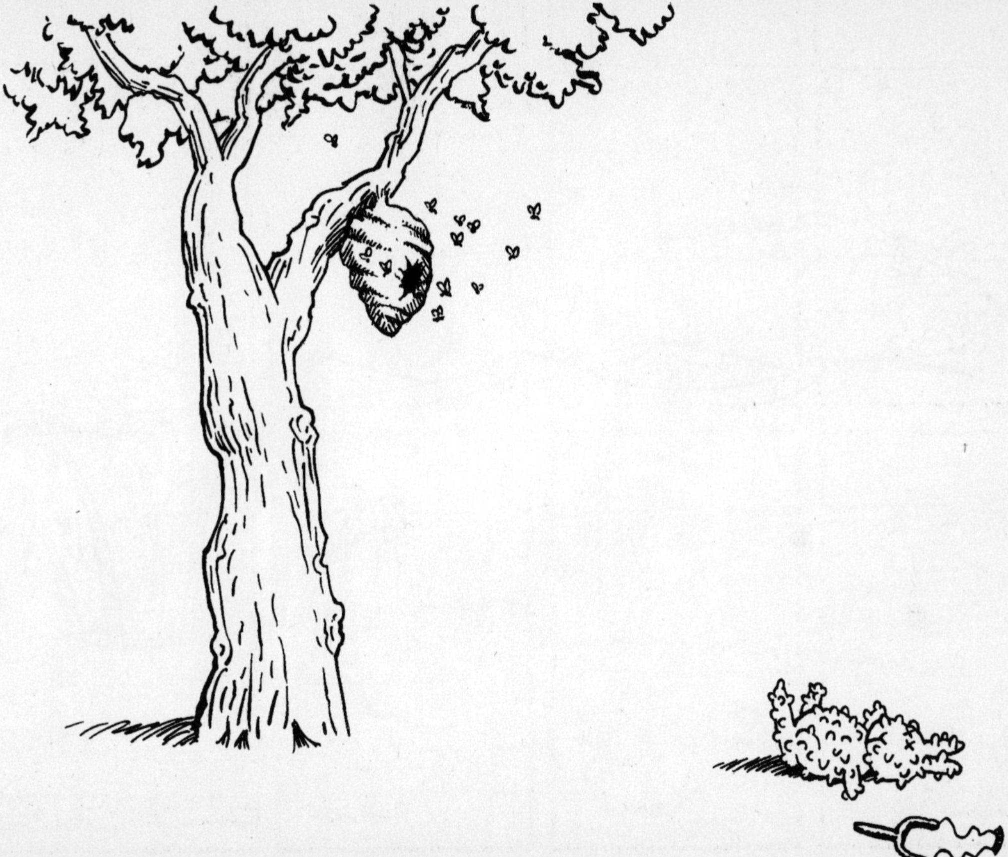

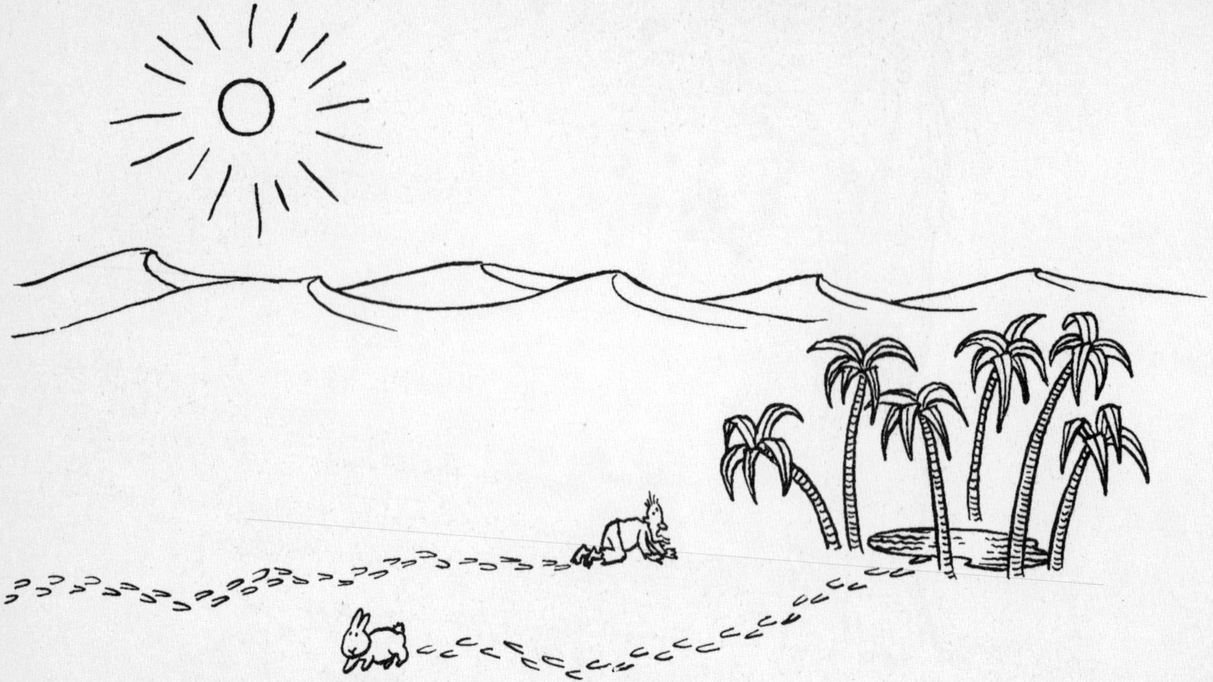

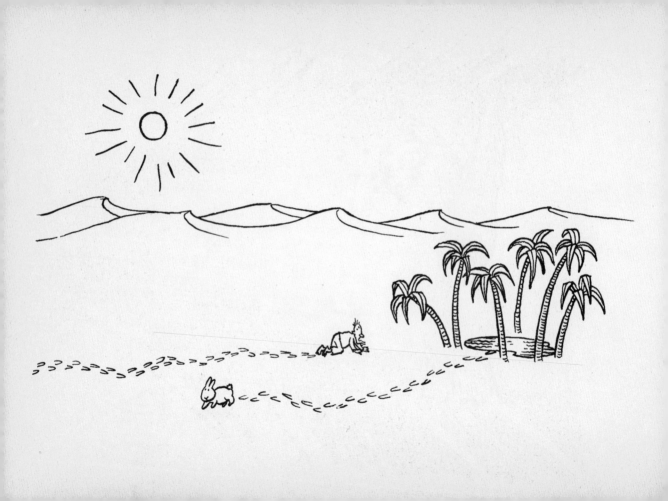

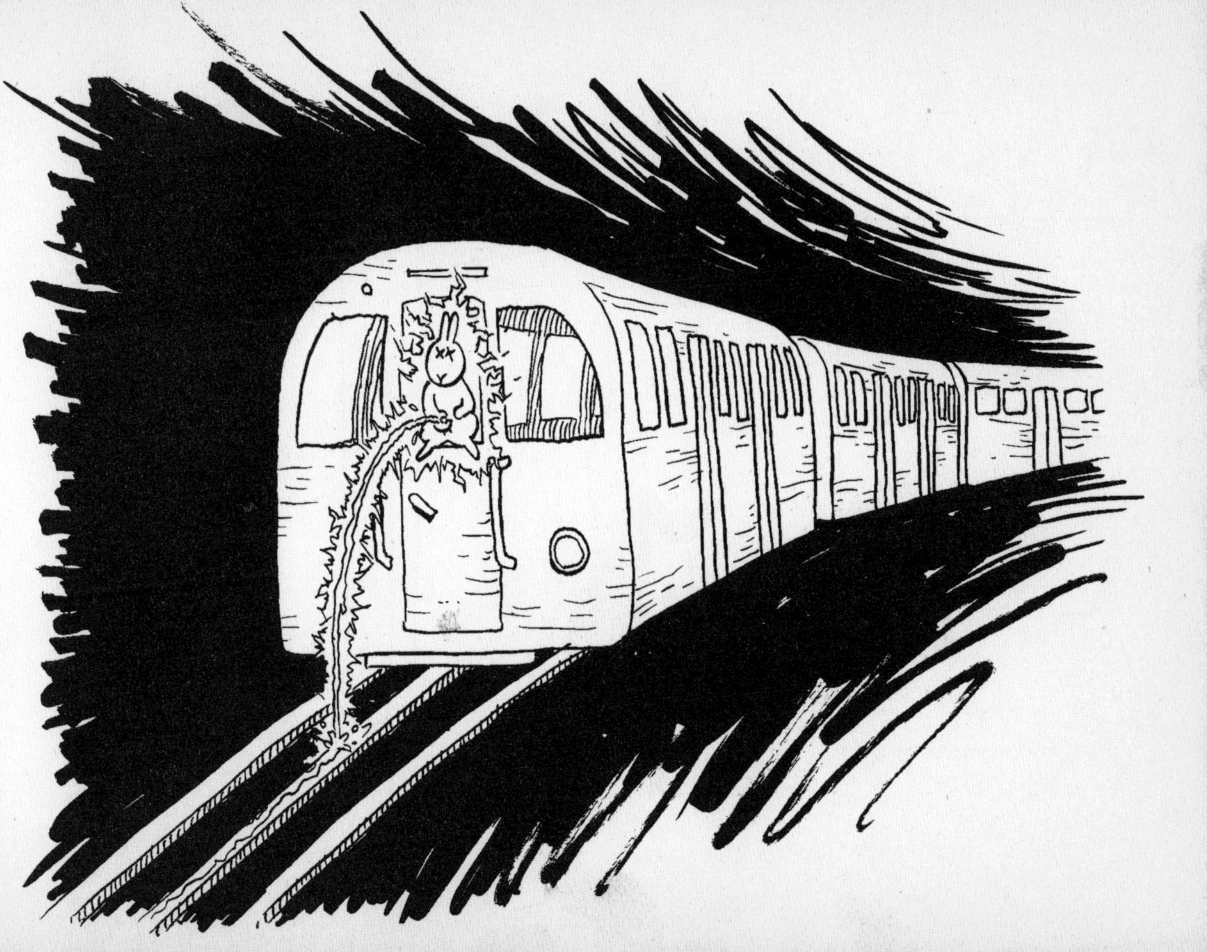

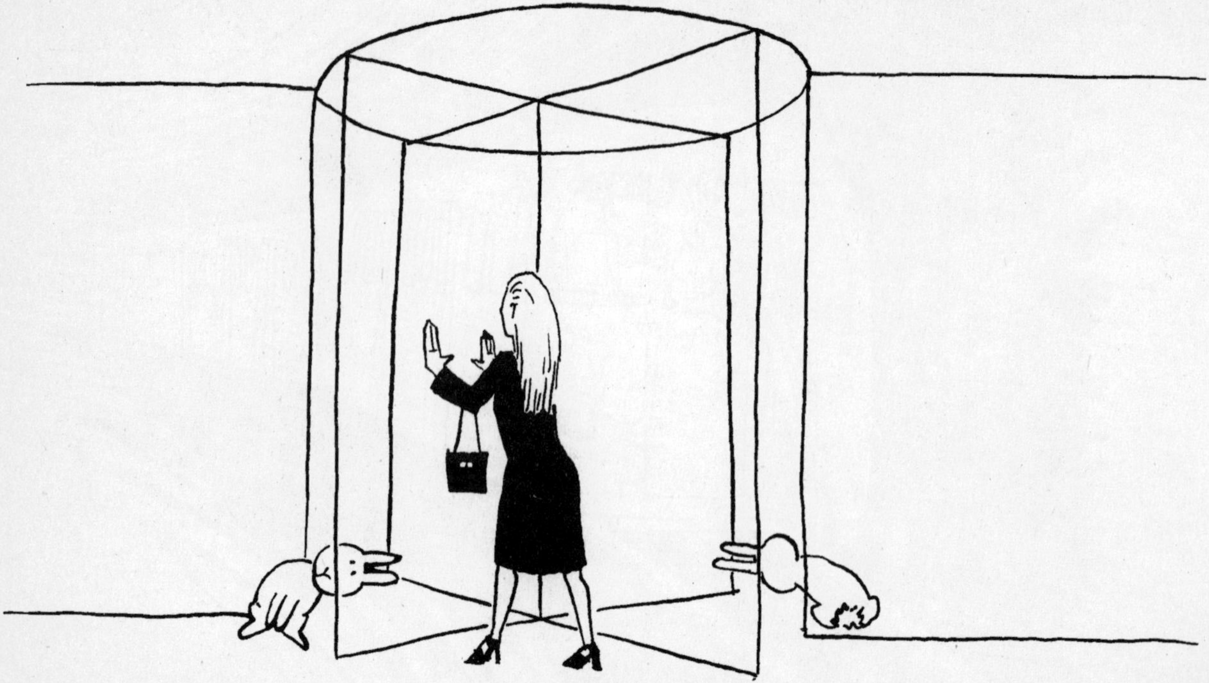

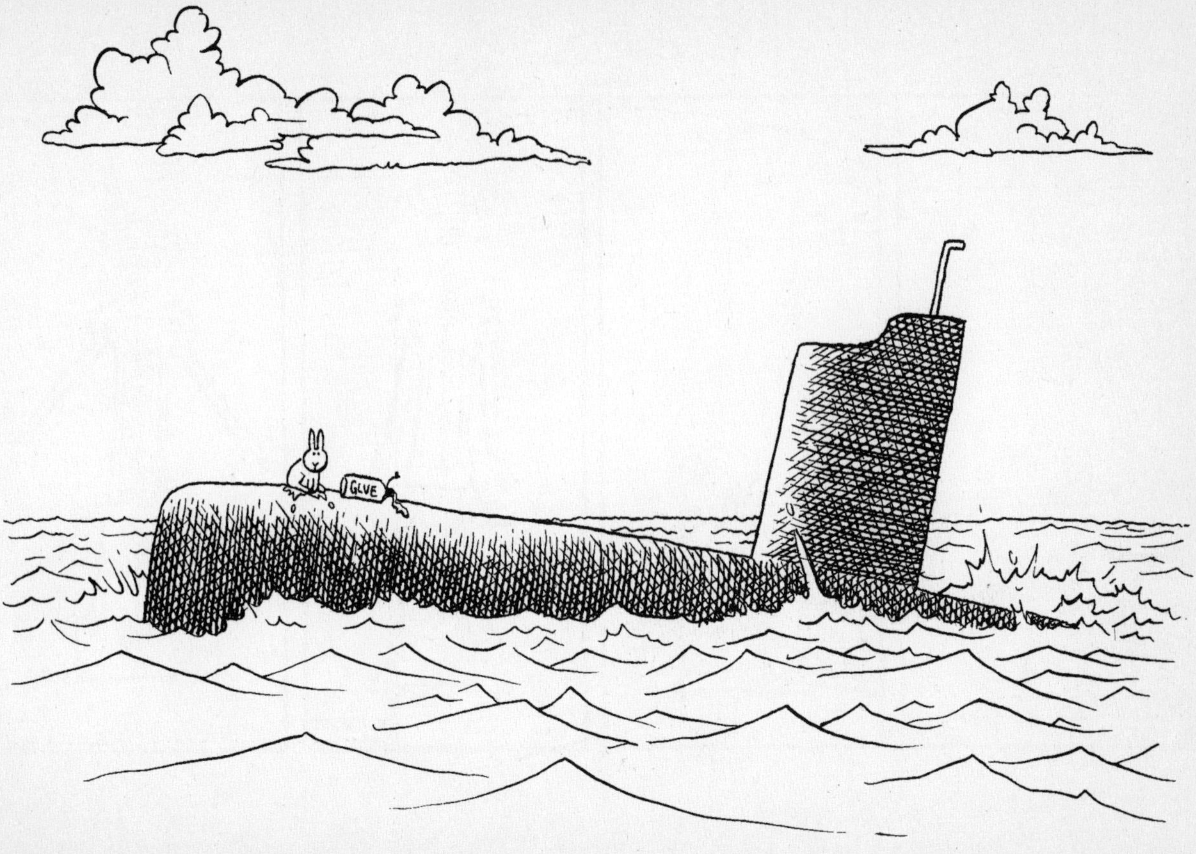
GLUE

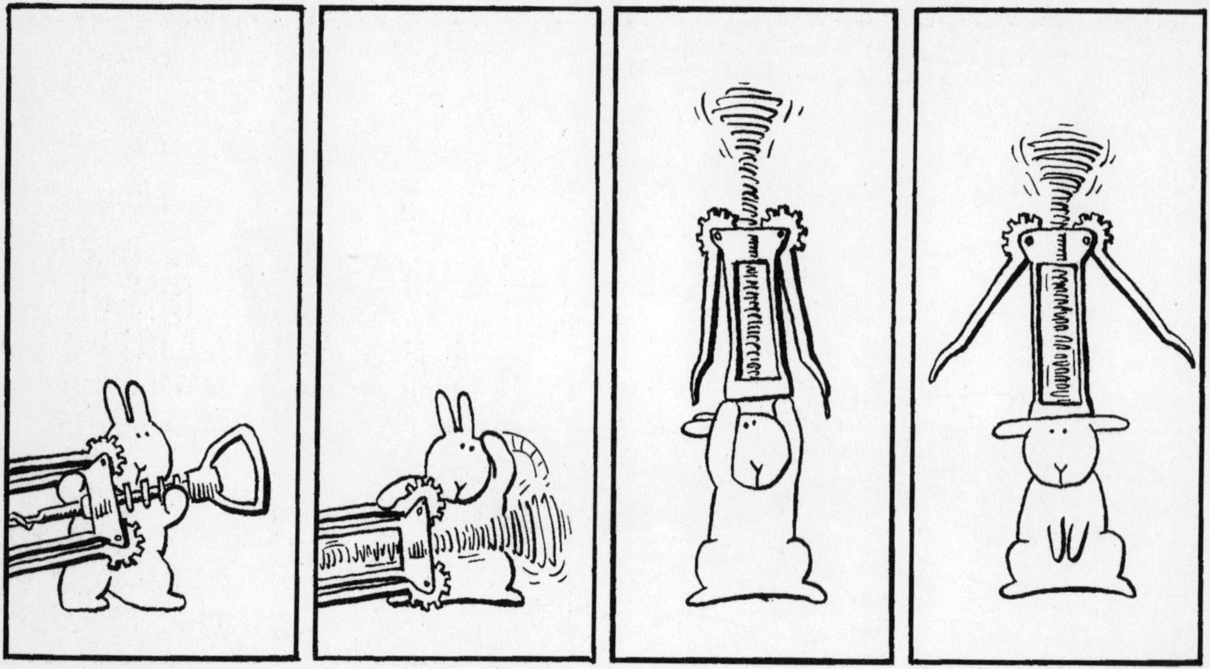

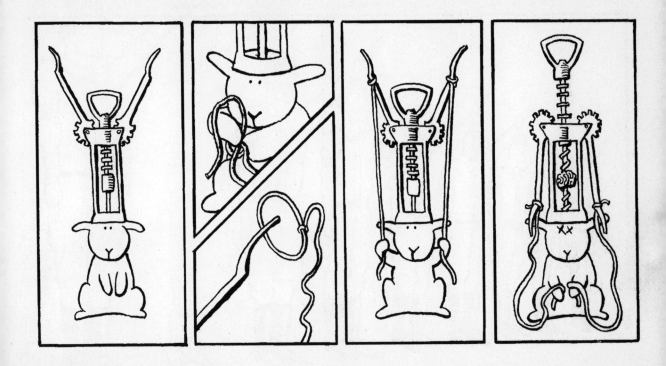

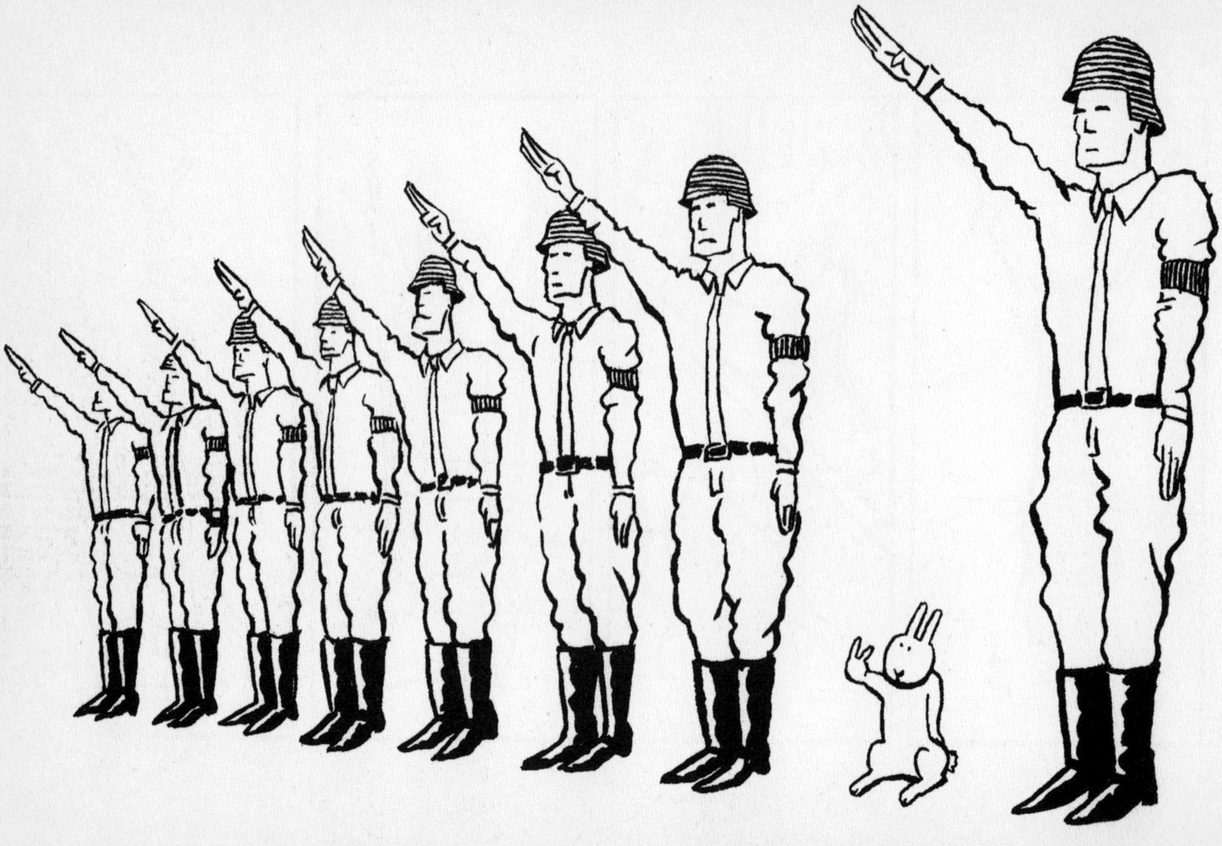

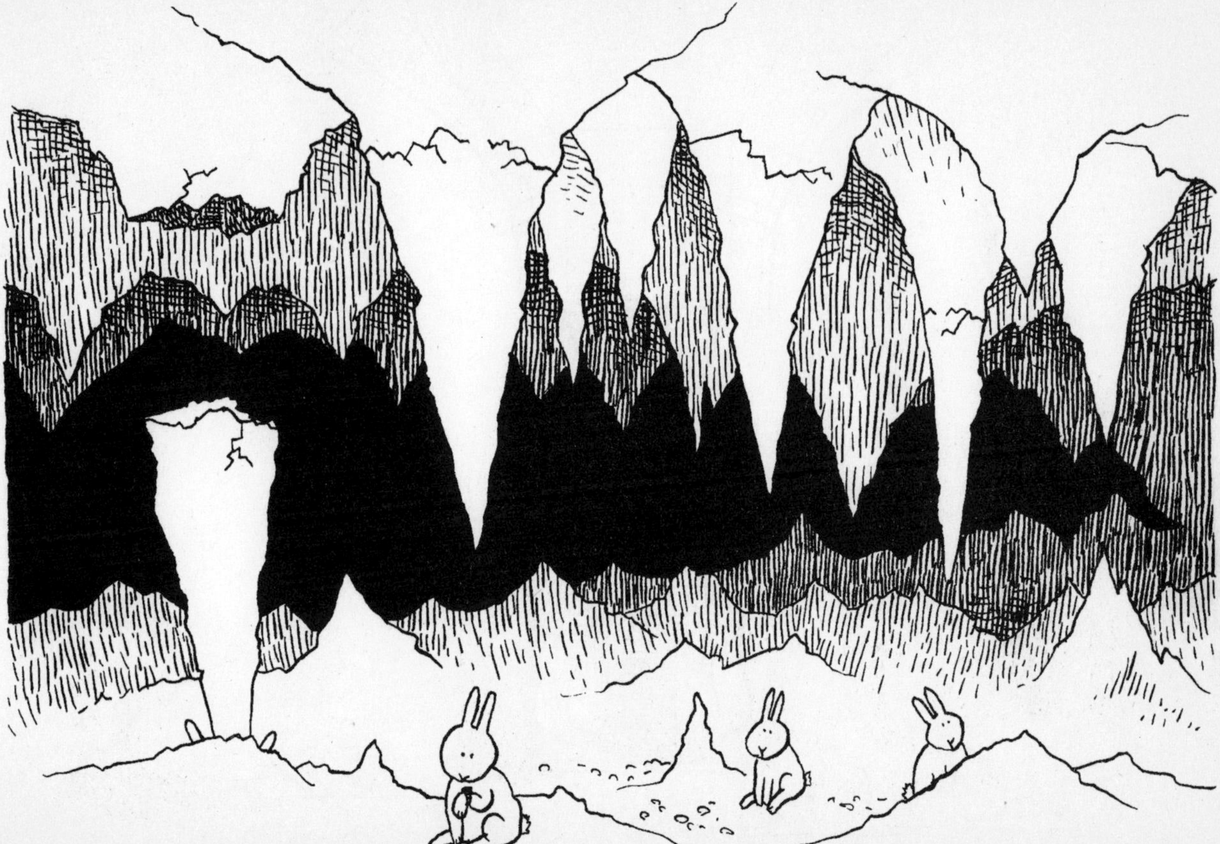

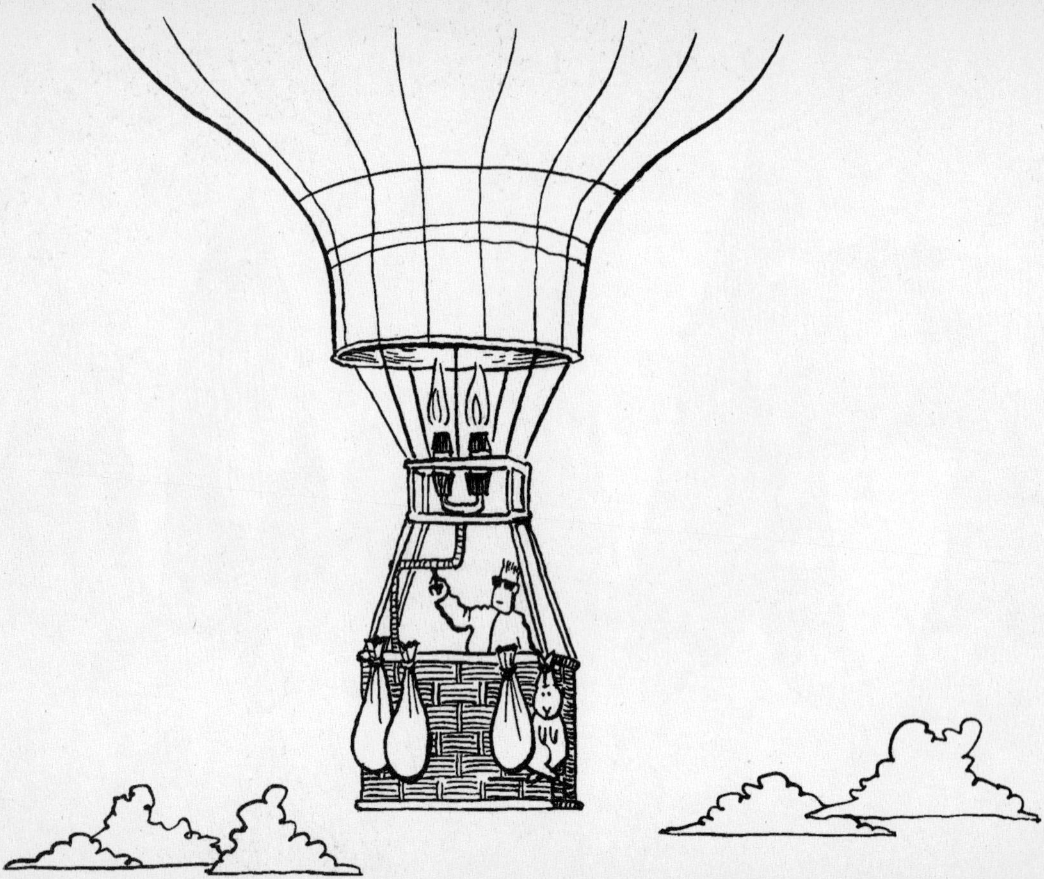

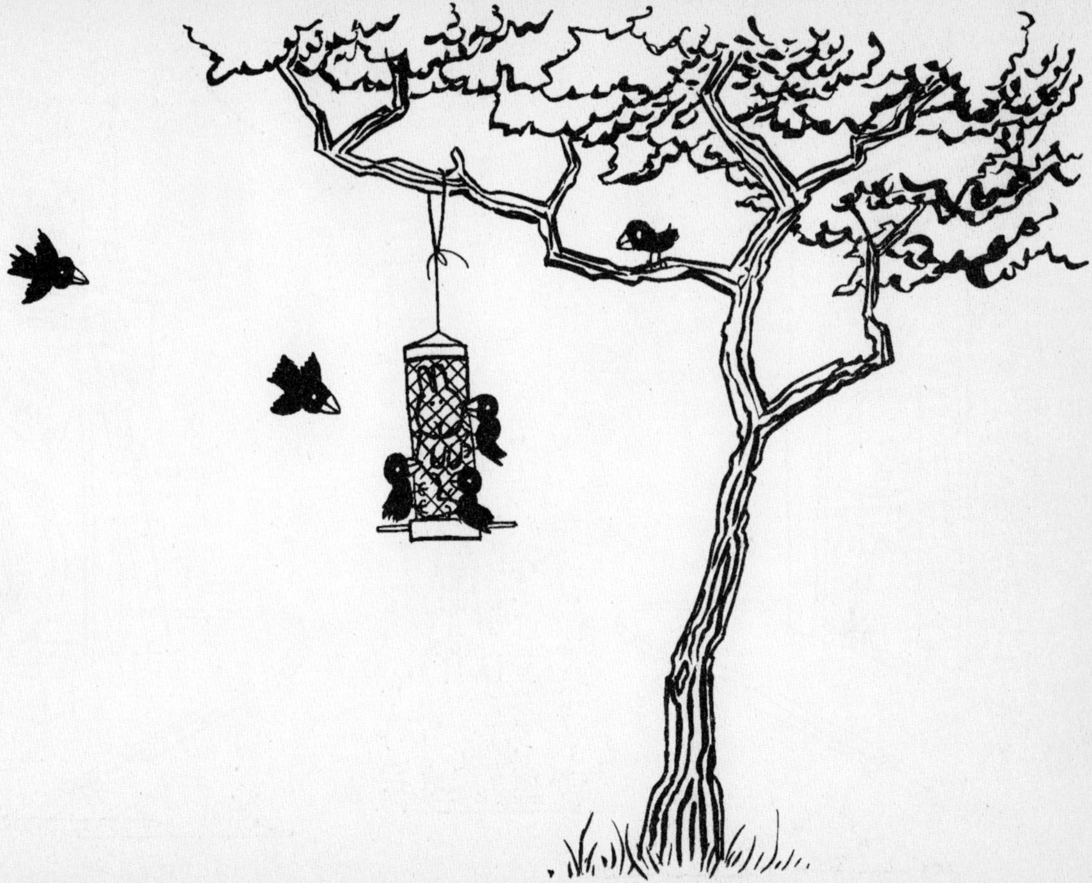

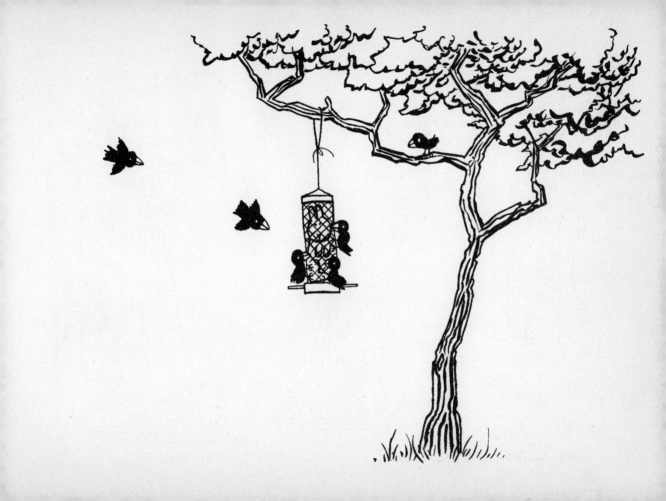

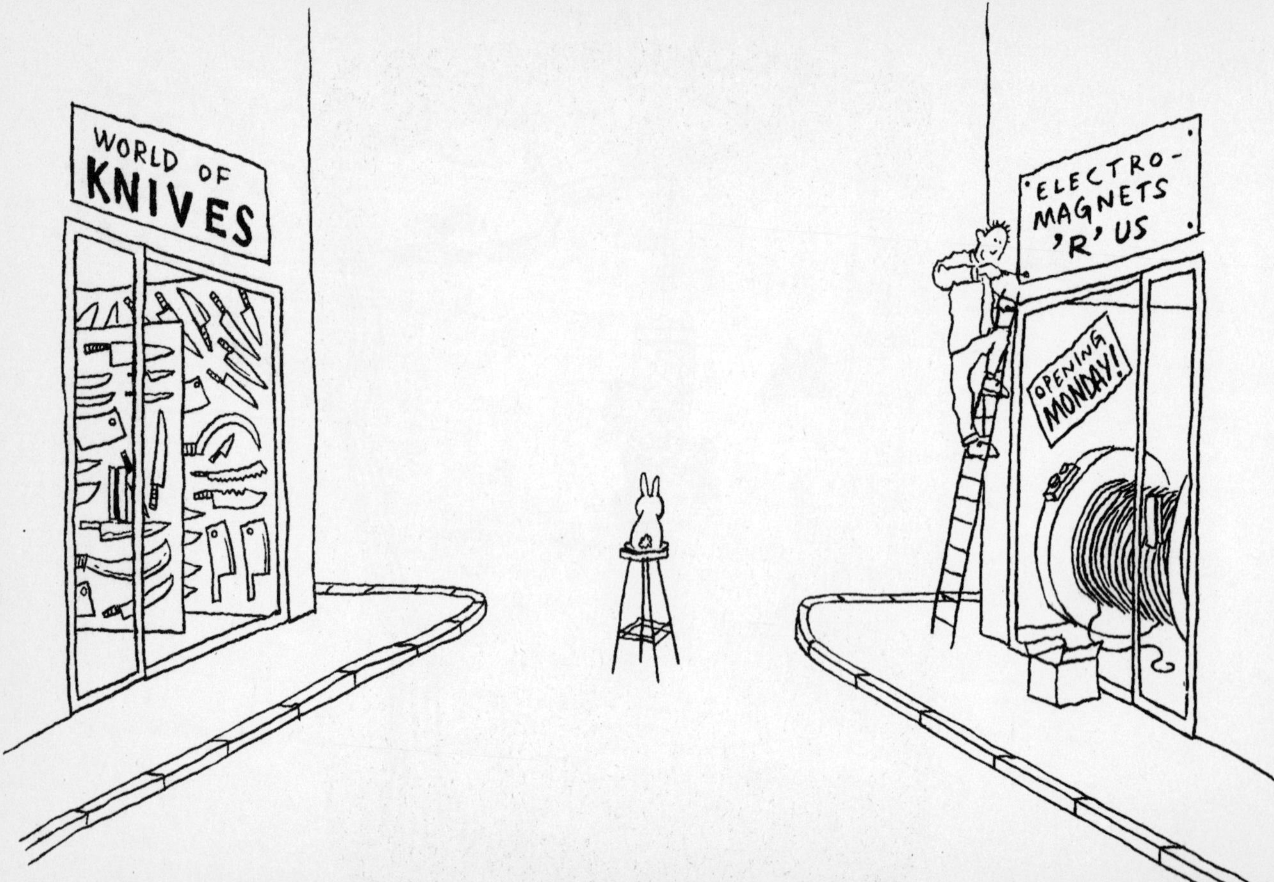
WORLD OF KNIVES
ELECTRO-MAGNETS 'R' US
OPENING MONDAY!

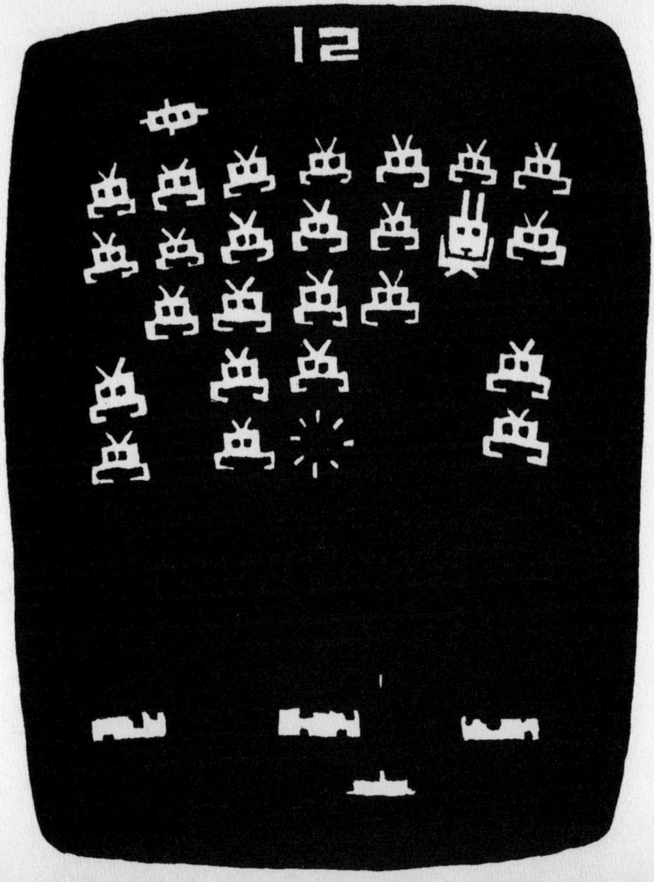
12

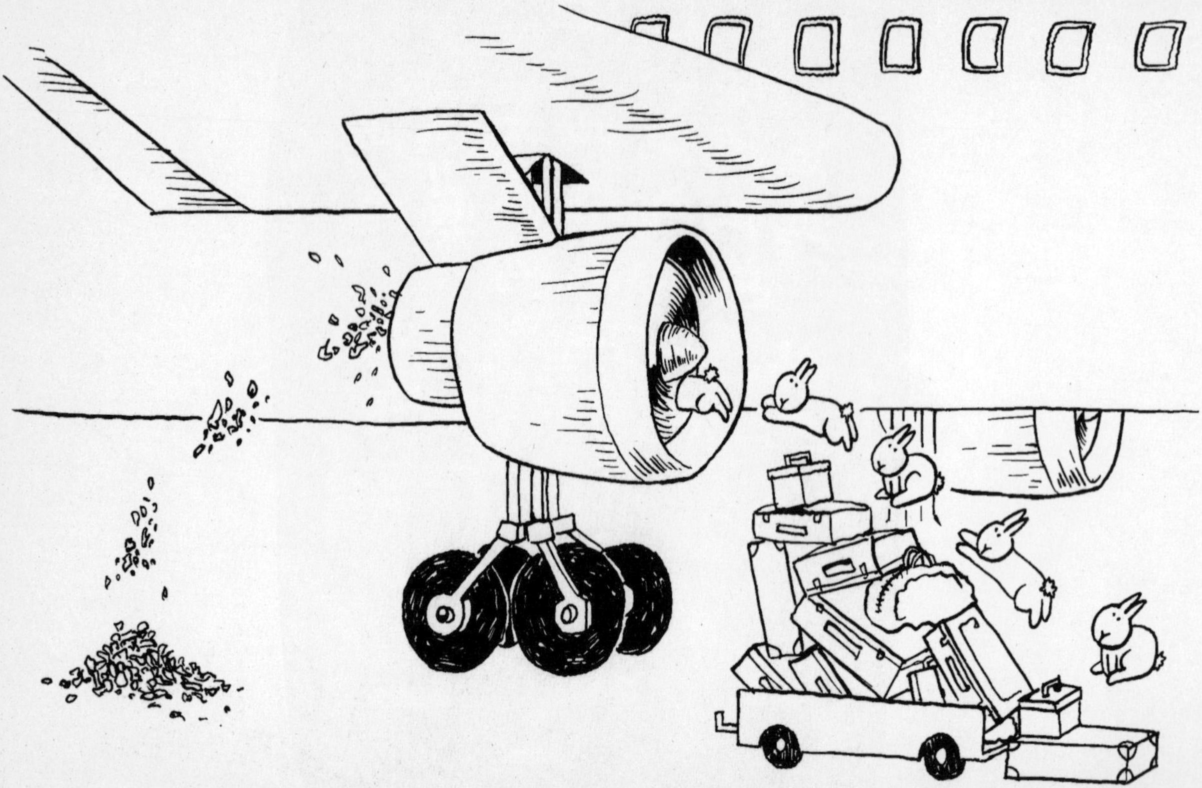

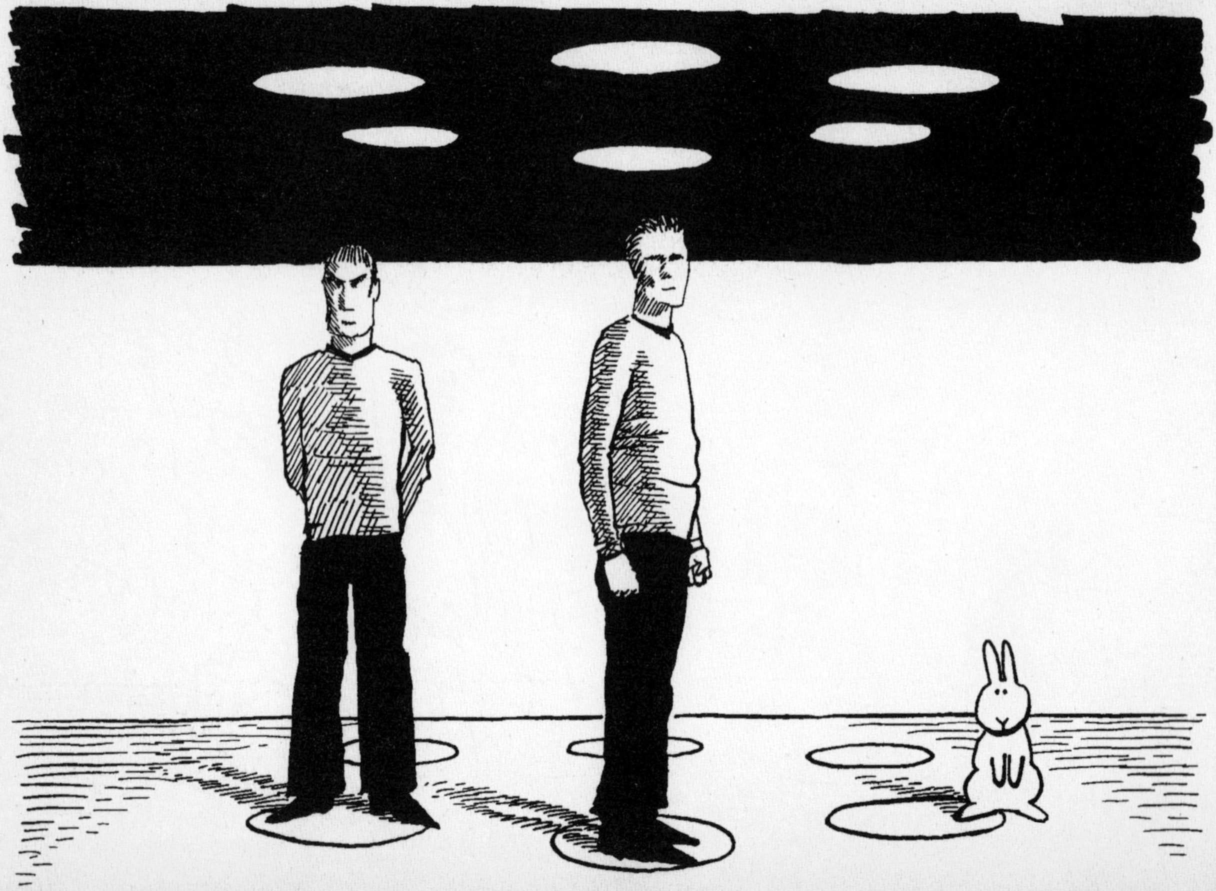

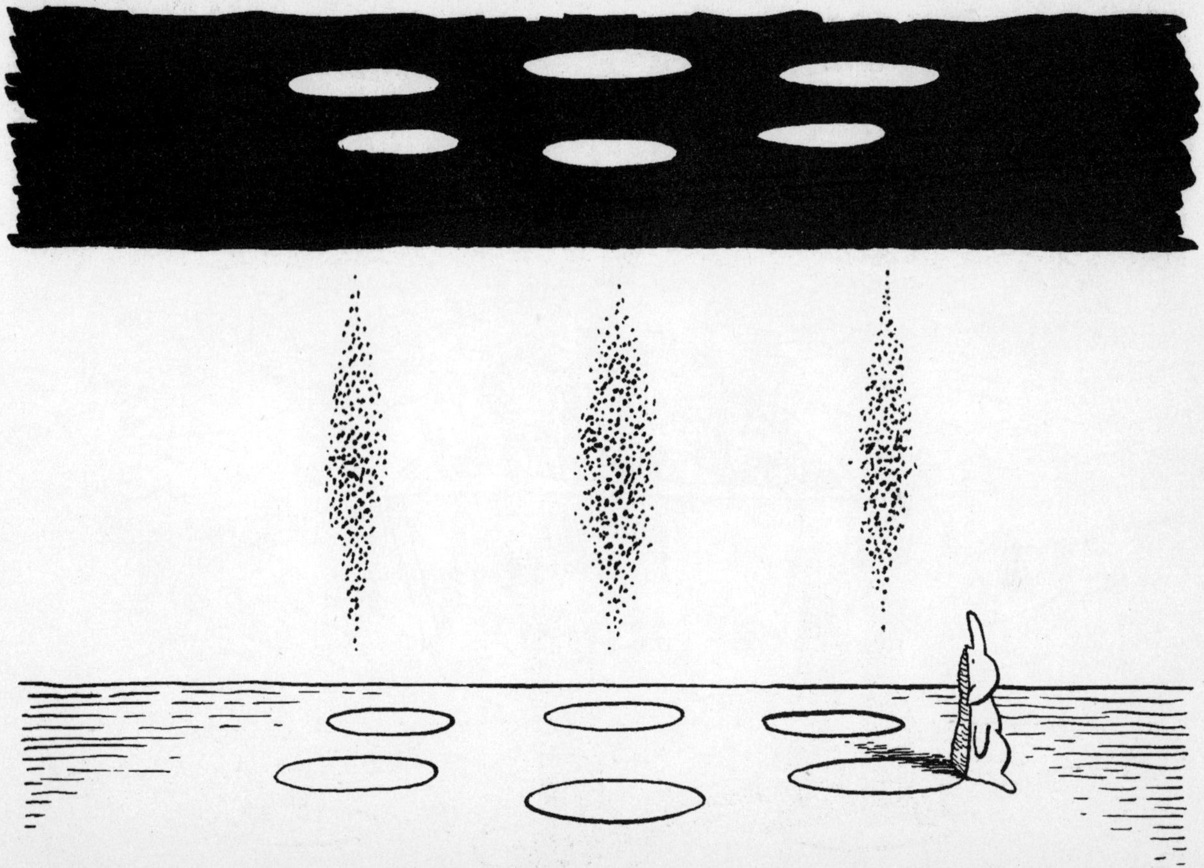

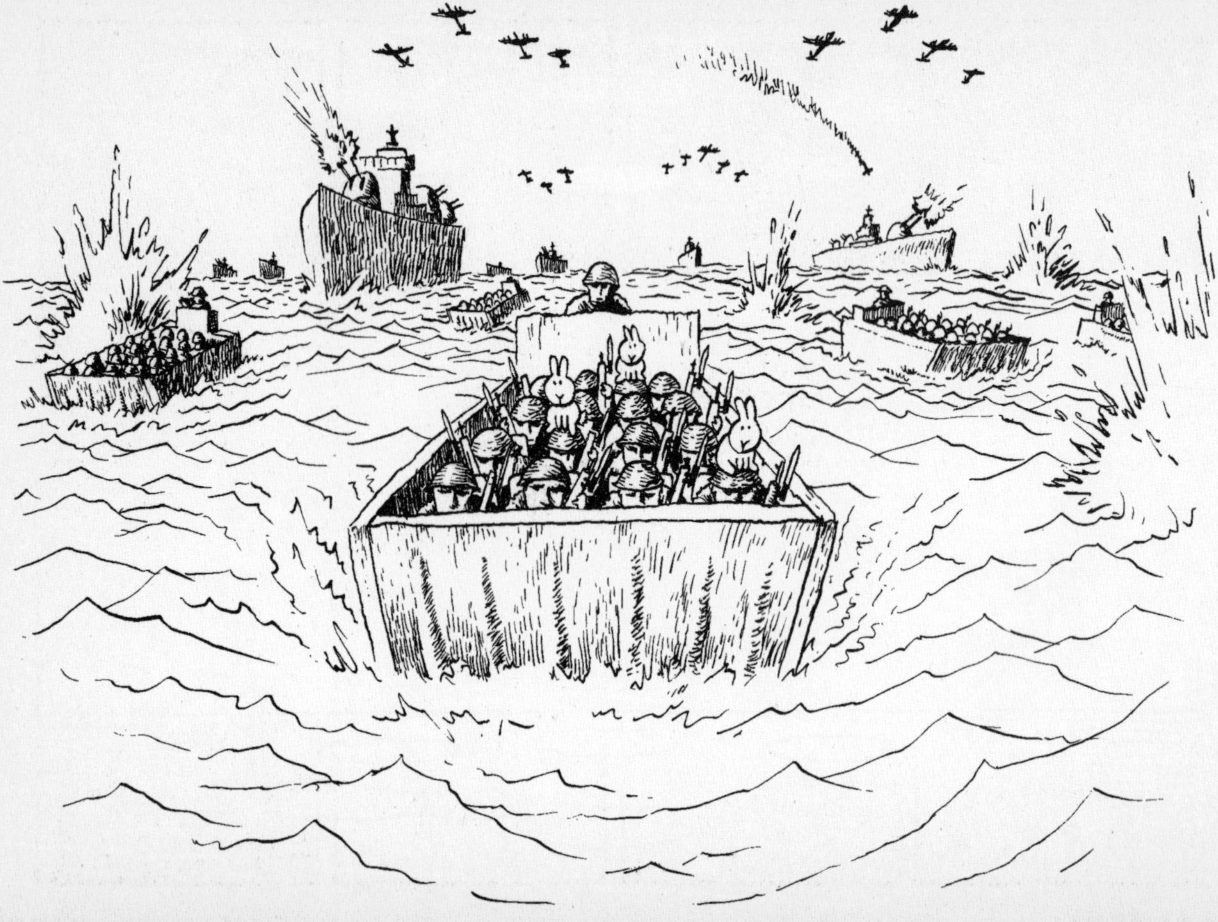

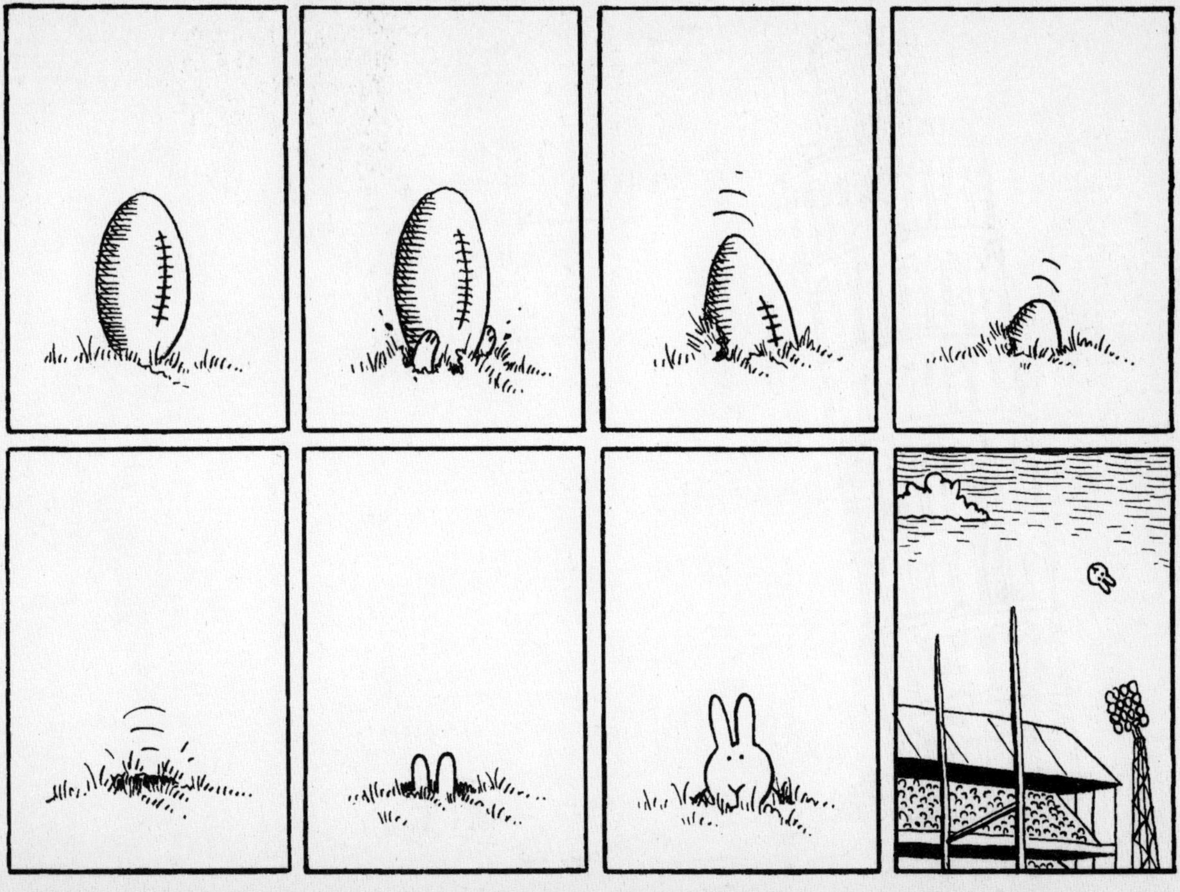

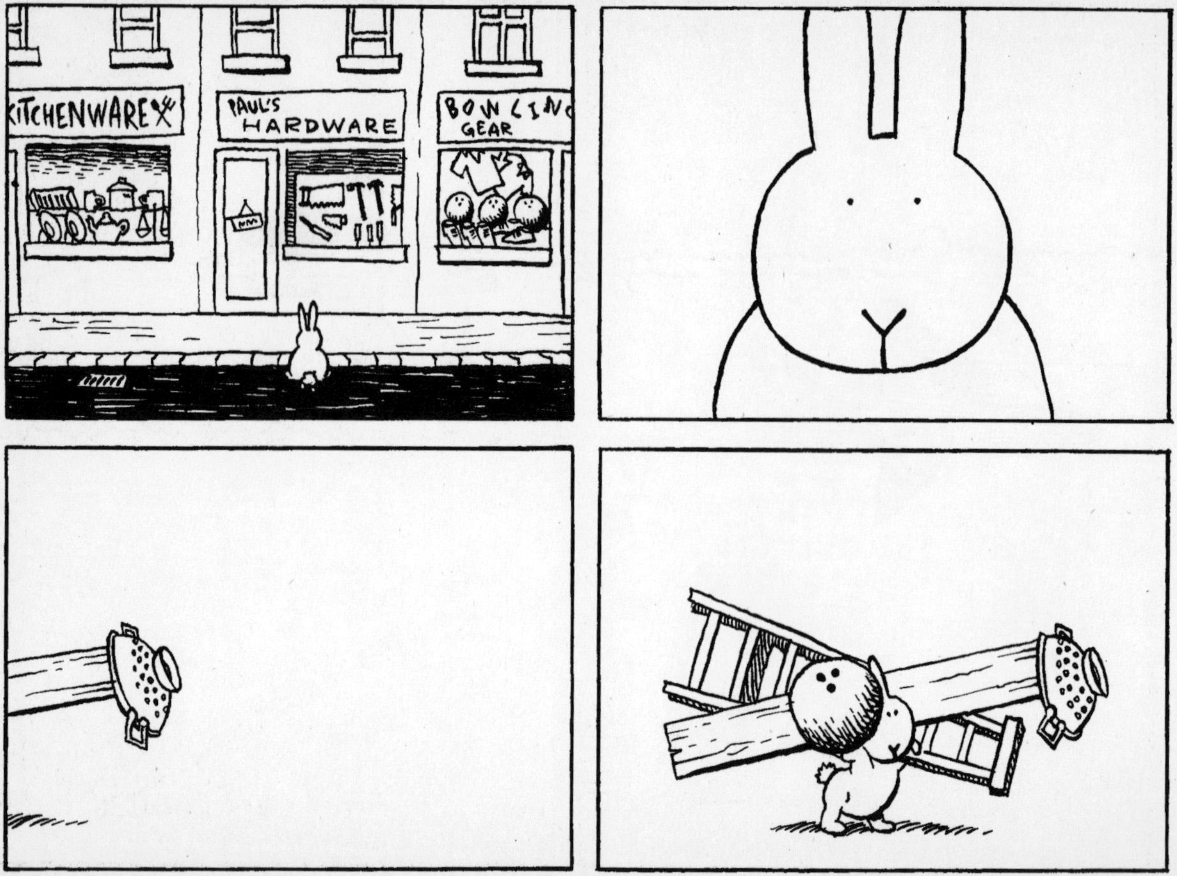
KITCHENWARE
PAUL'S
HARDWARE
BOWLING
GEAR

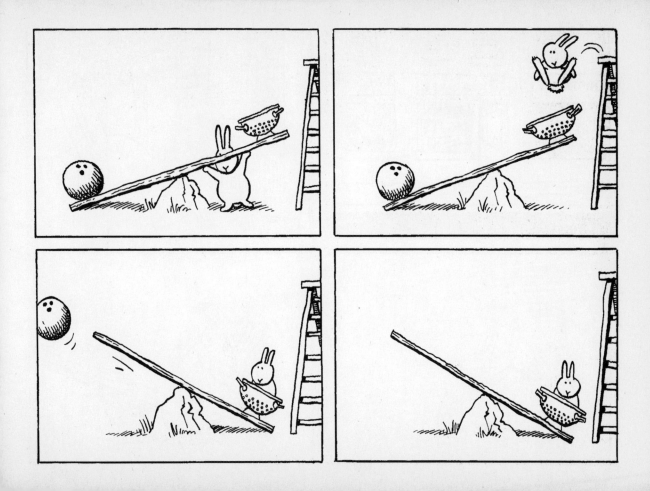

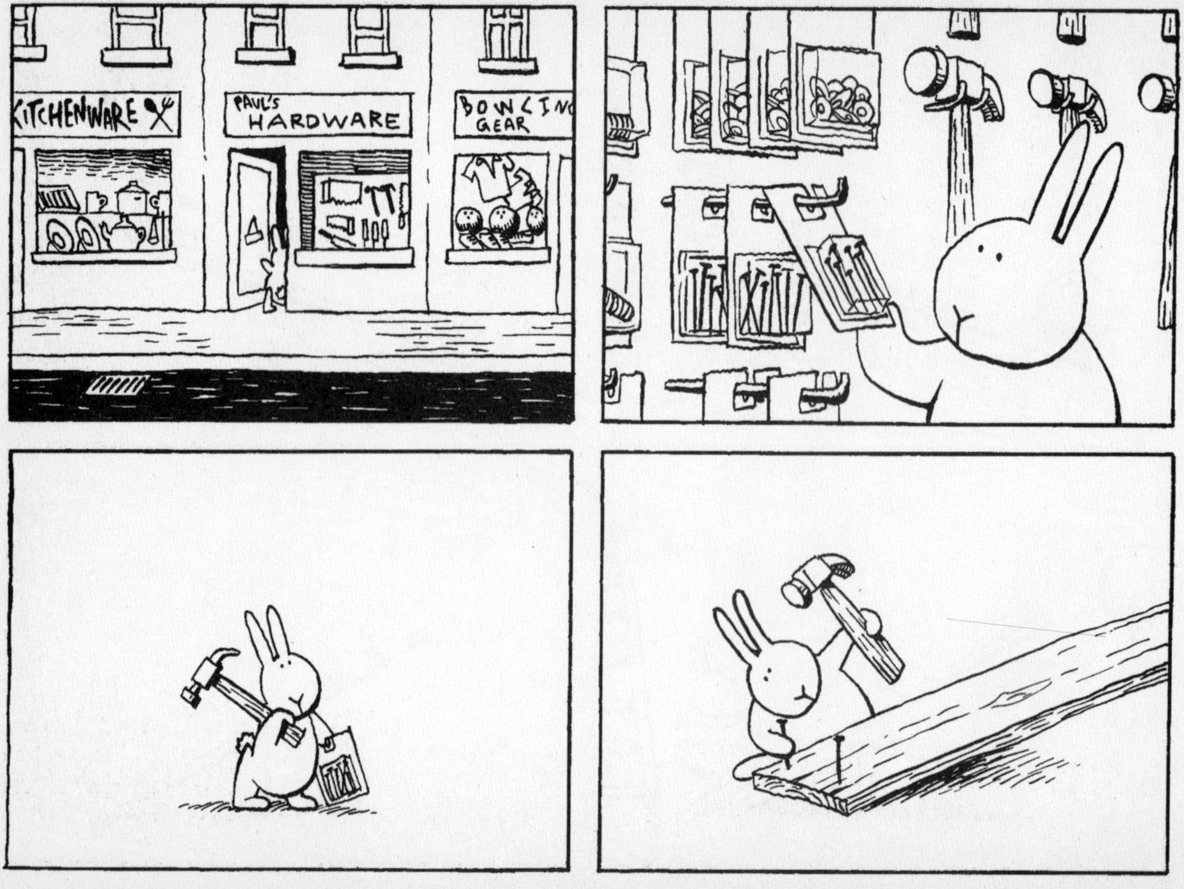
KITCHENWARE
PAUL'S HARDWARE
BOWLING GEAR

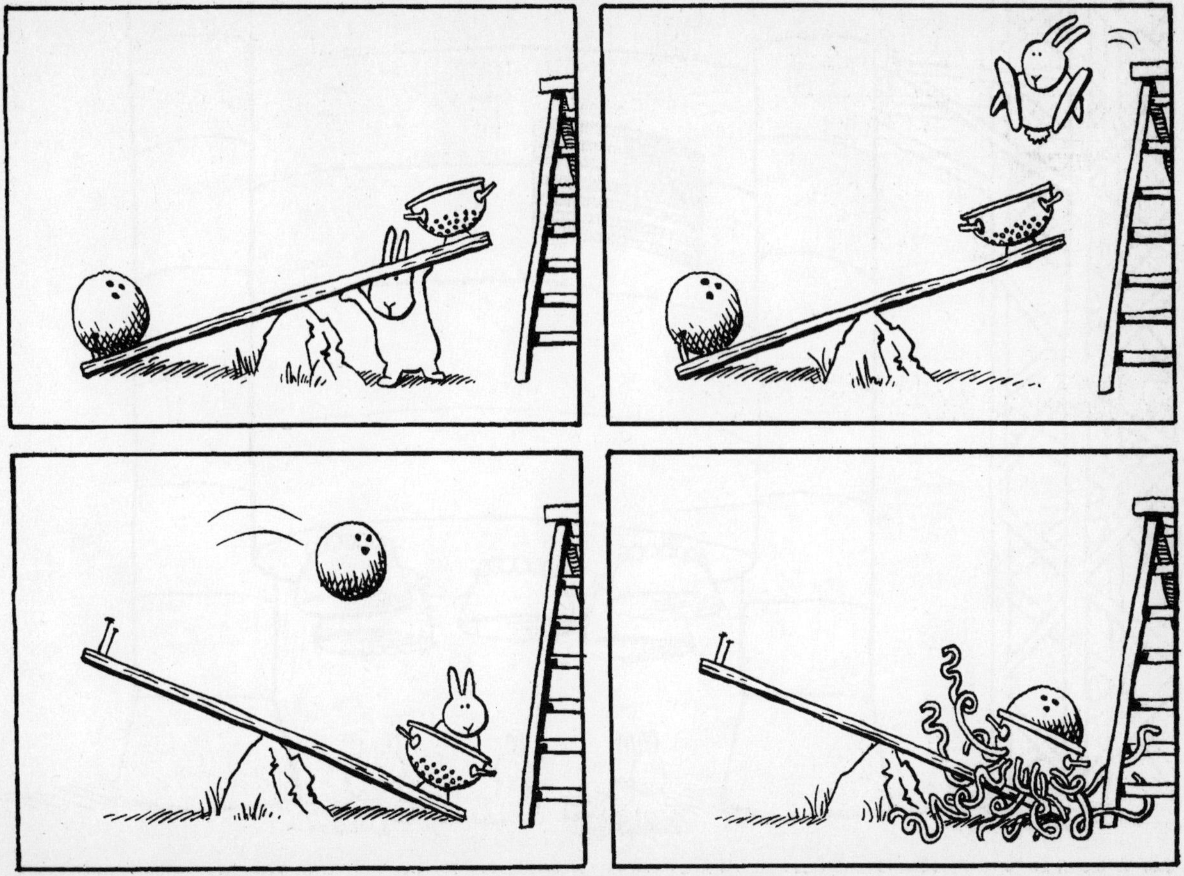

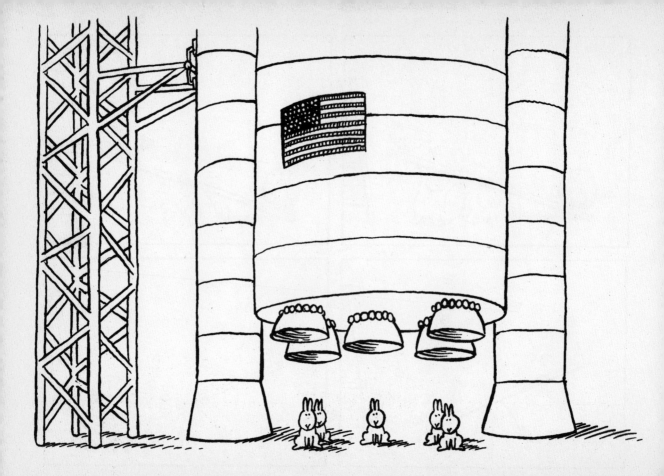

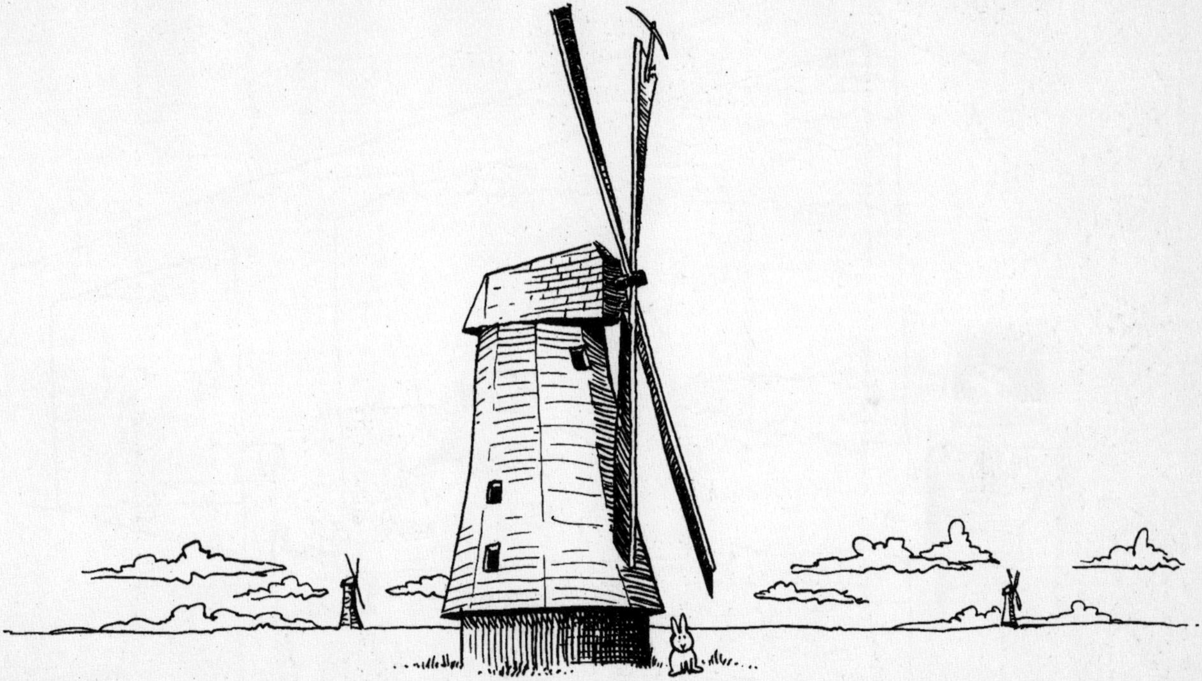

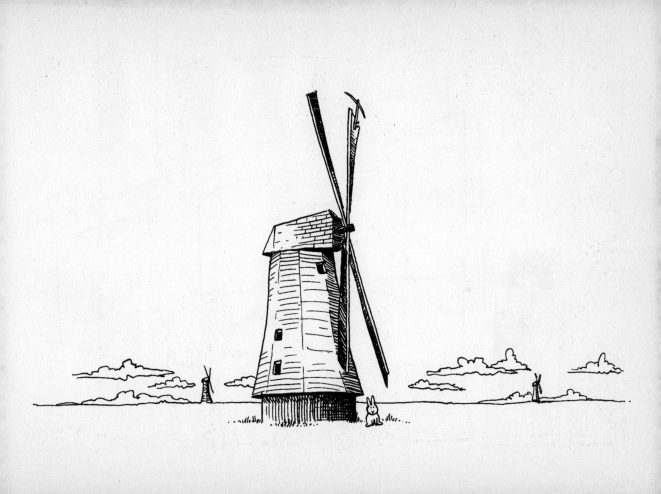

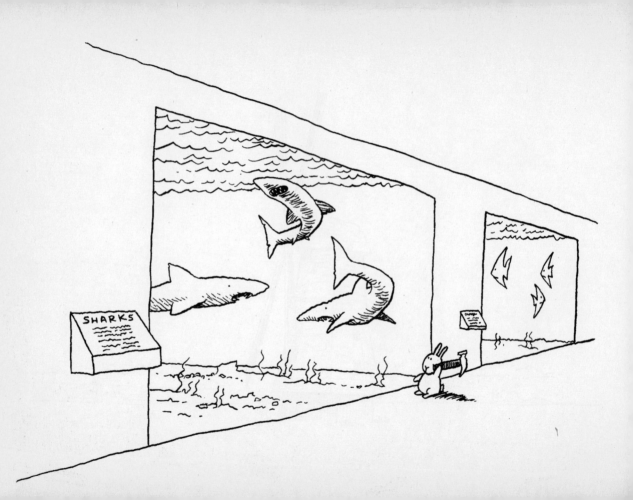

SHARKS

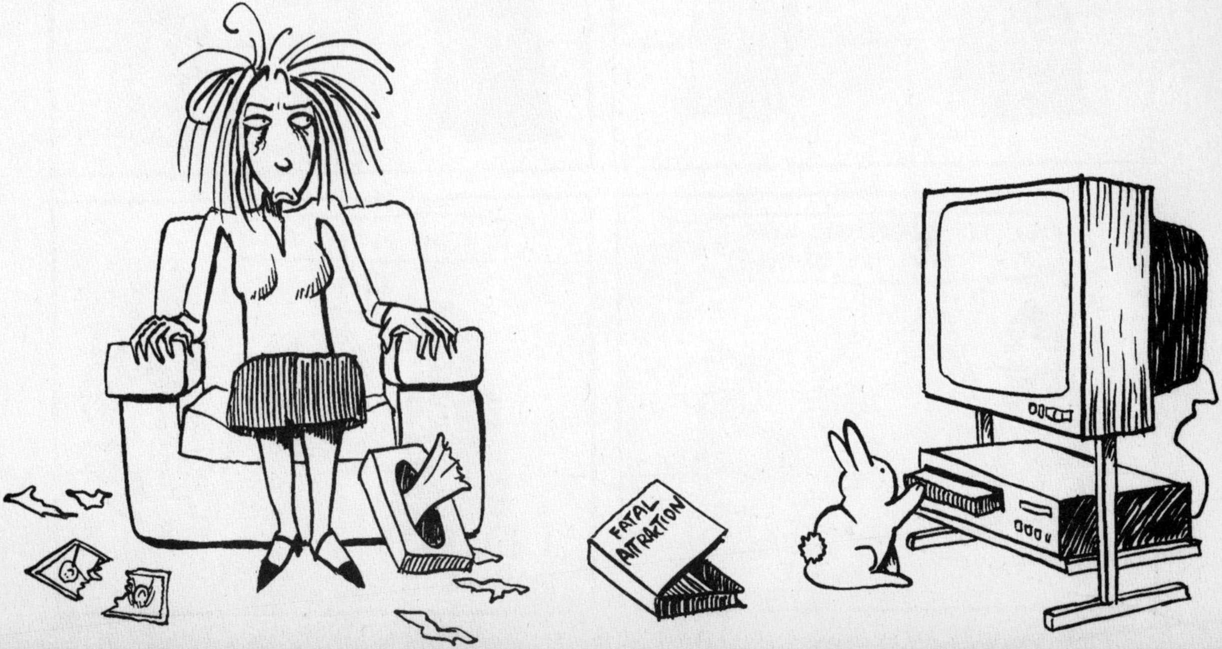
FATAL ATTRACTION

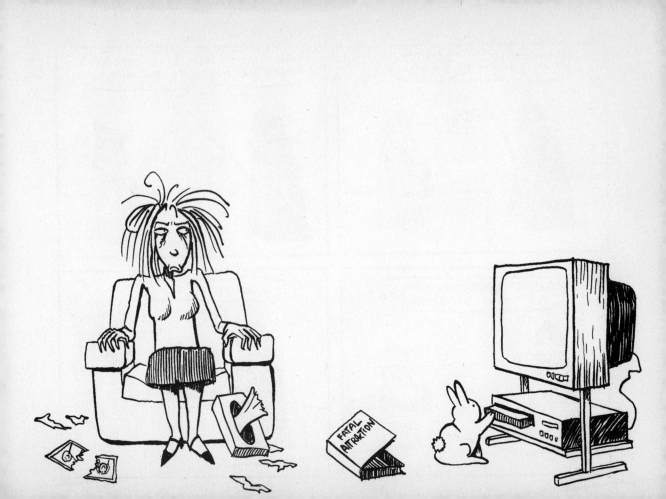

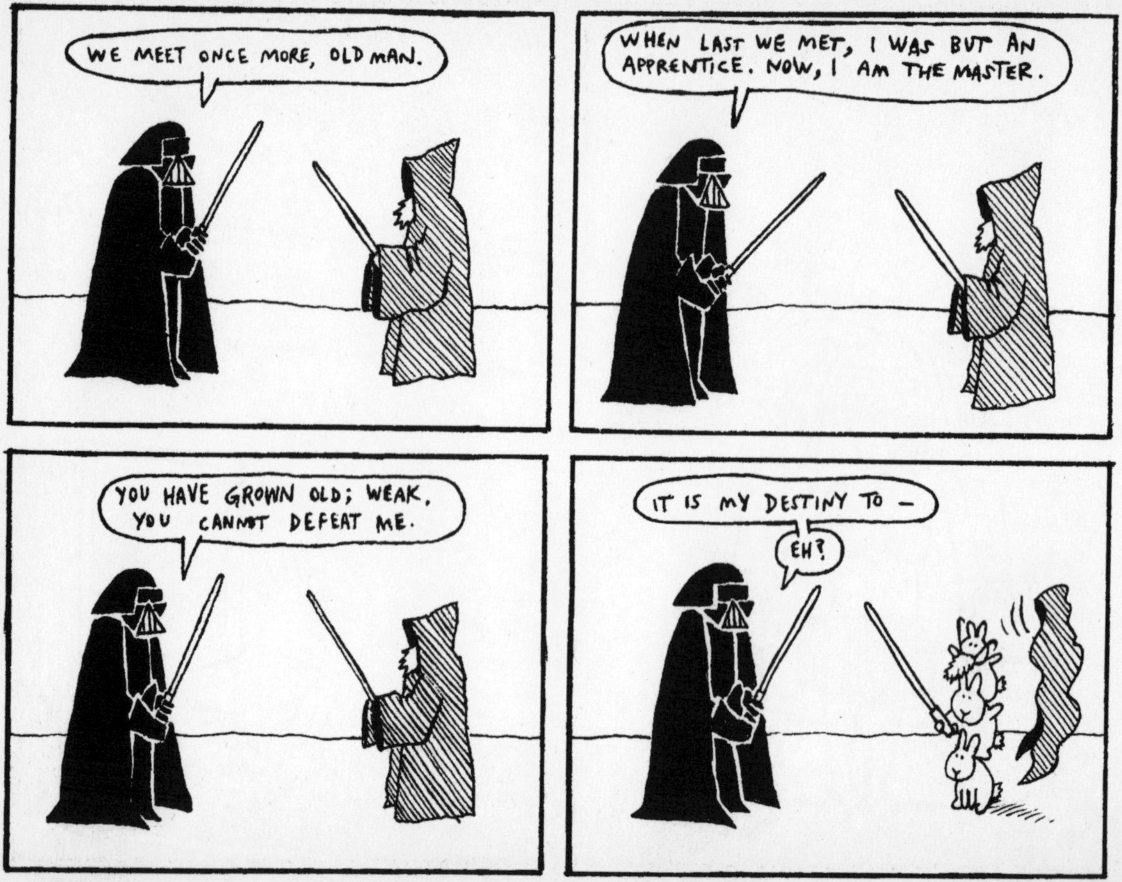
WE MEET ONCE MORE, OLD MAN.
WHEN LAST WE MET, I WAS BUT AN APPRENTICE. NOW, I AM THE MASTER.
YOU HAVE GROWN OLD; WEAK. YOU CANNOT DEFEAT ME.
IT IS MY DESTINY TO –
EH?

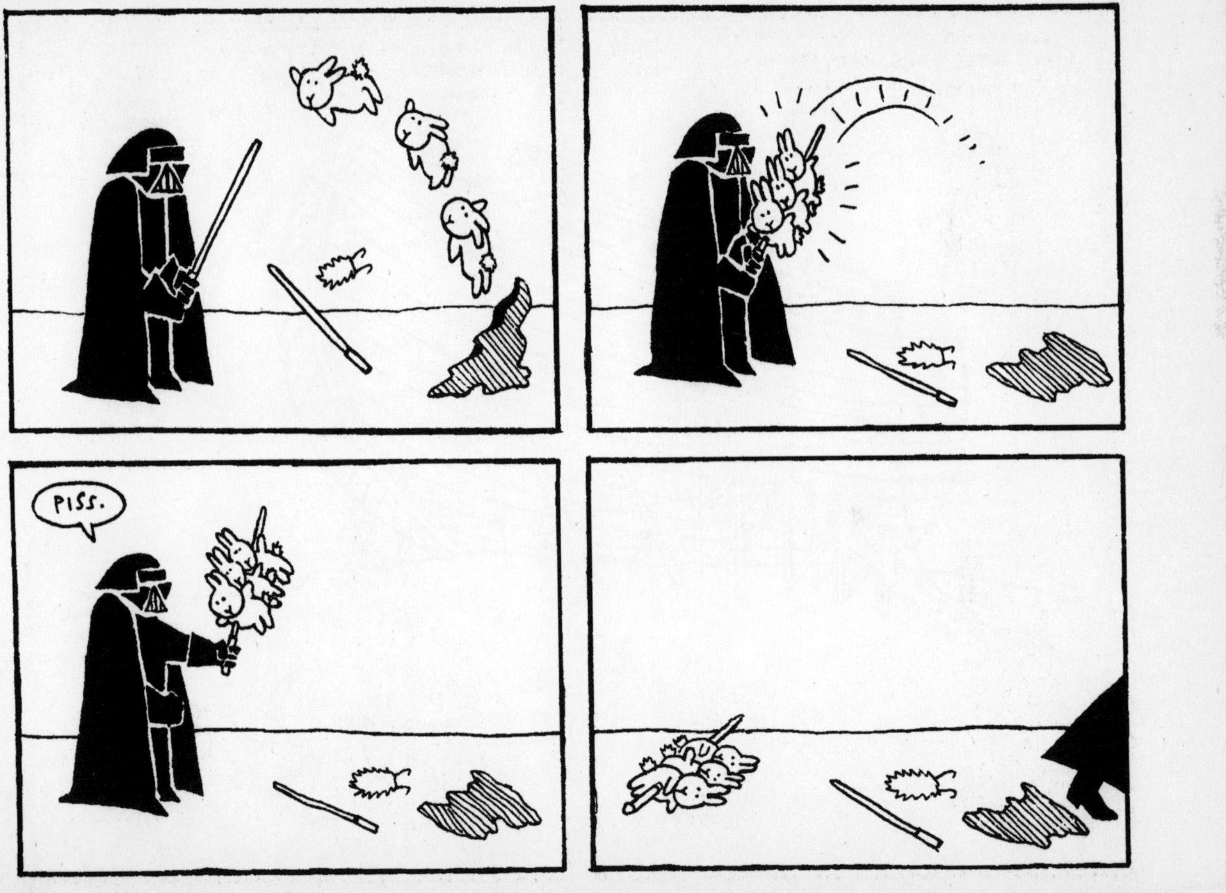
PISS.

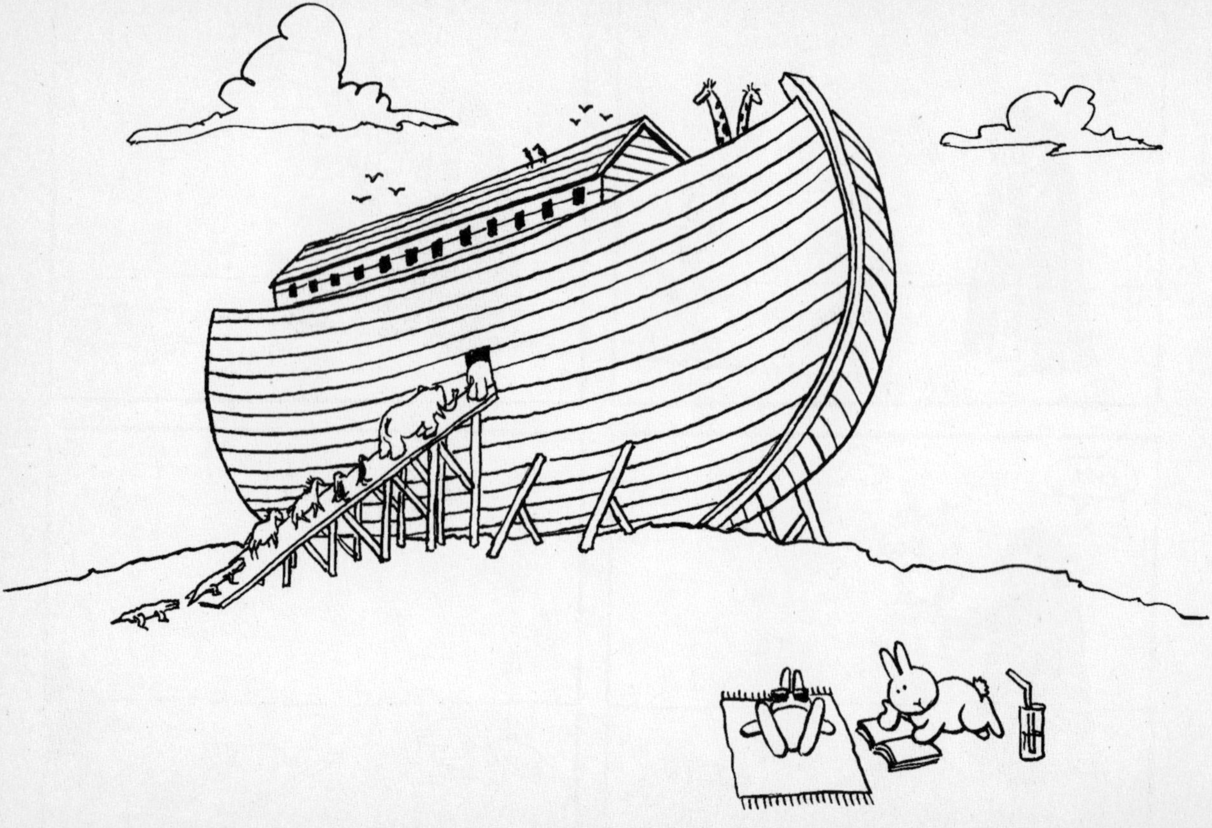

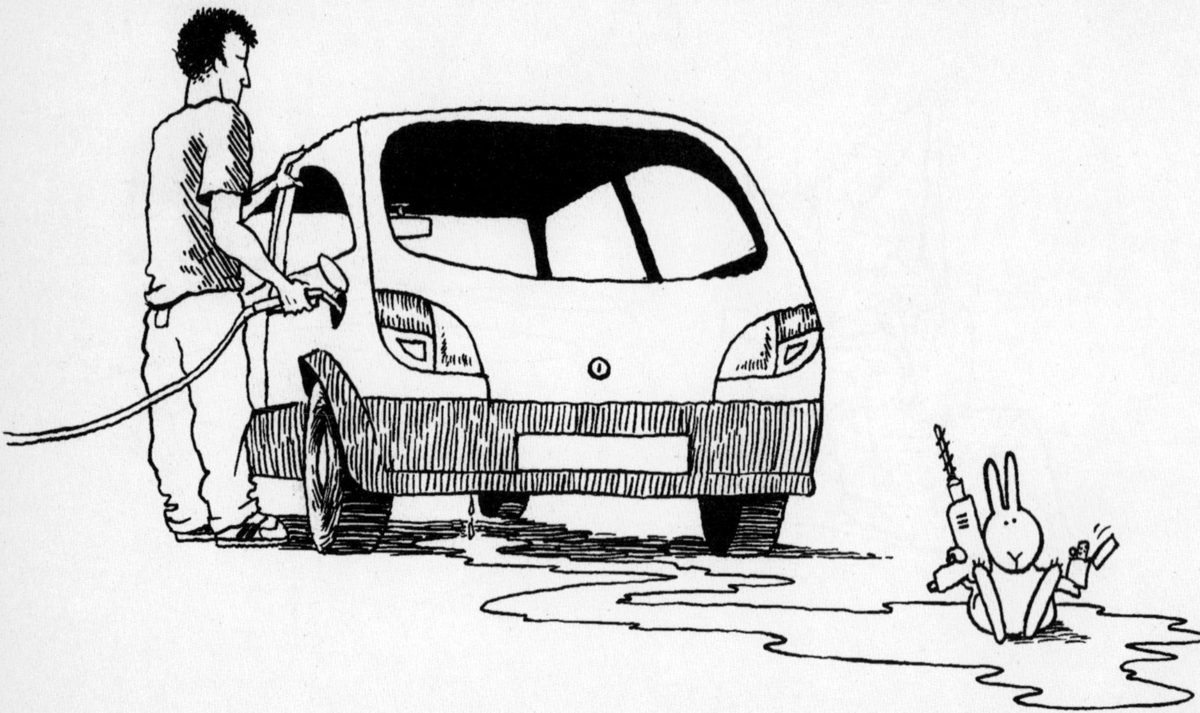

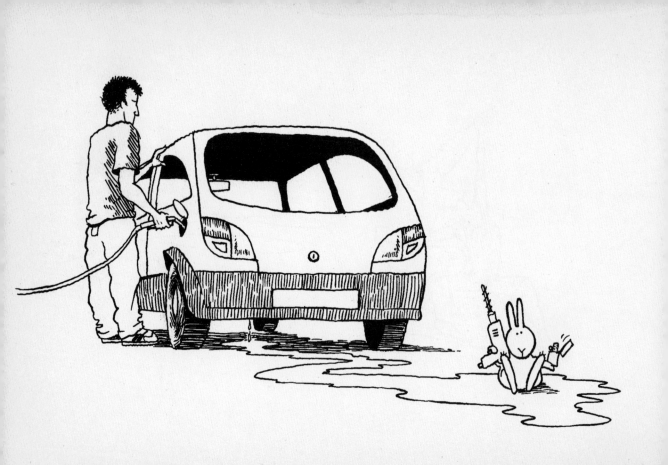

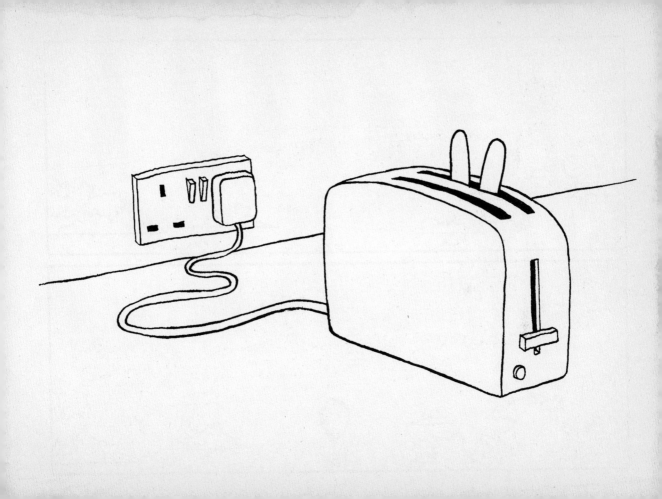

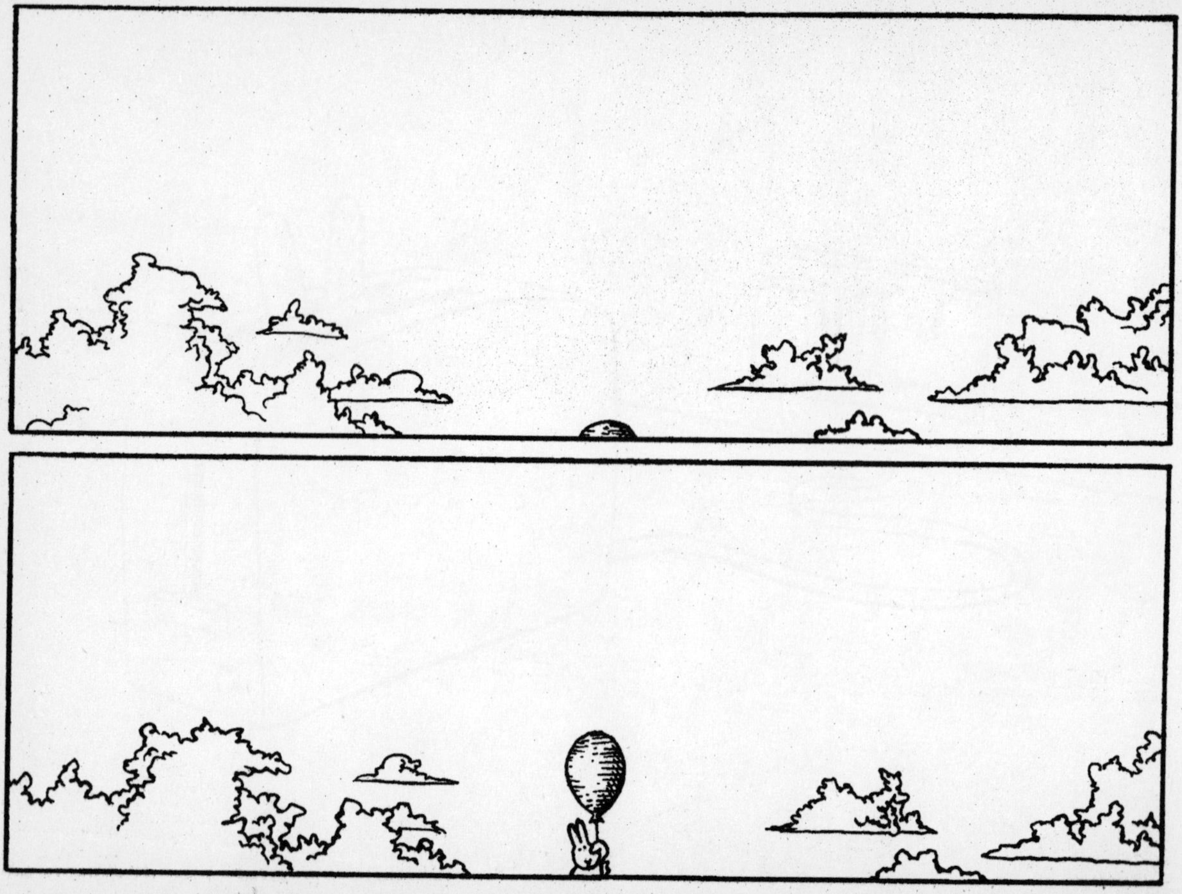

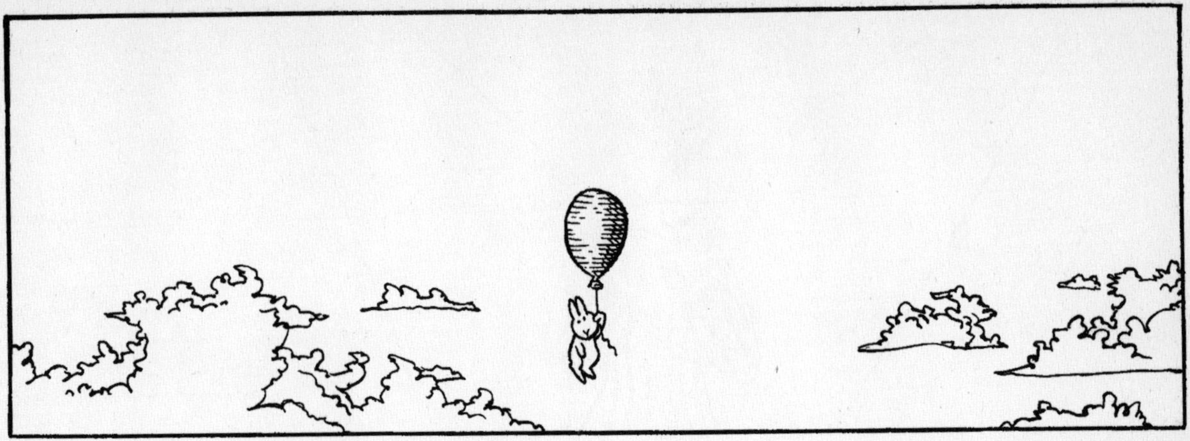

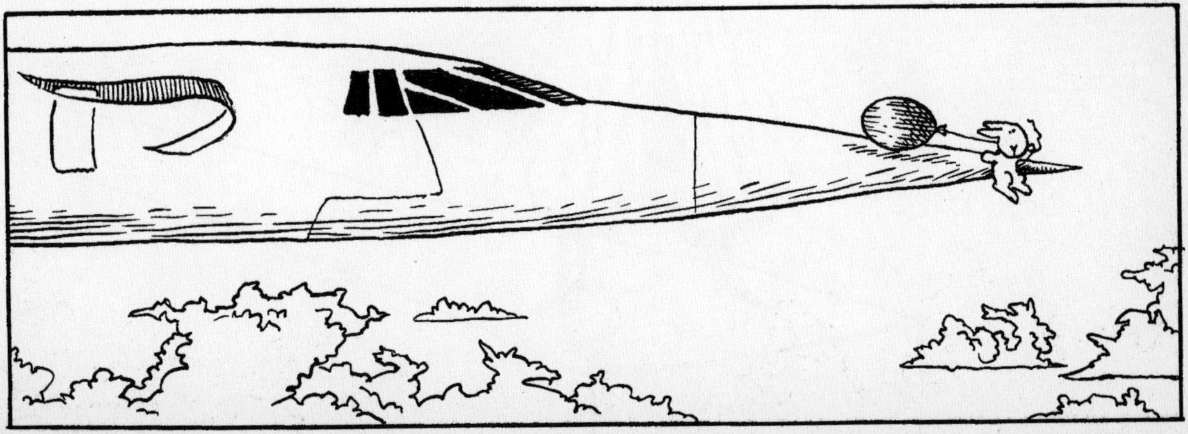

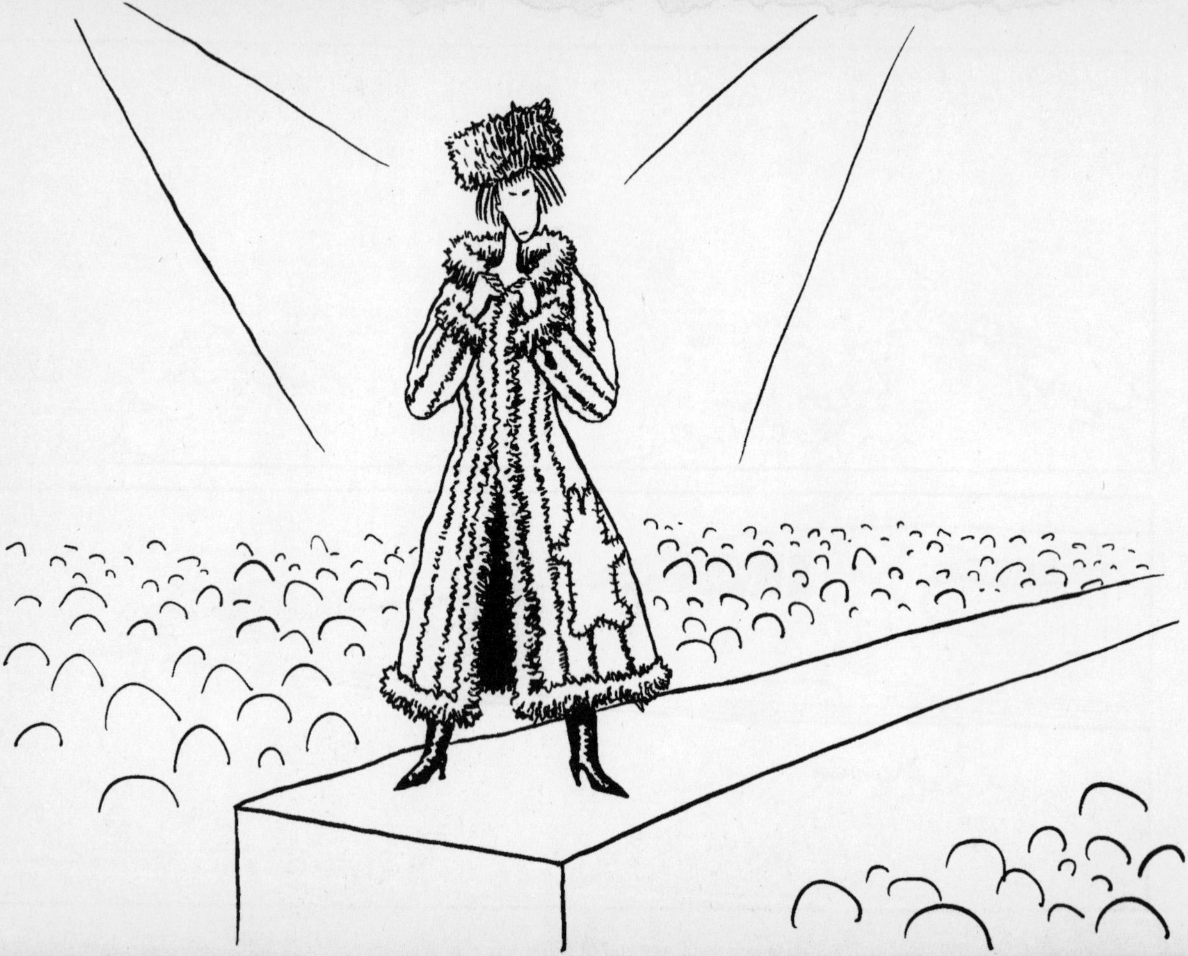

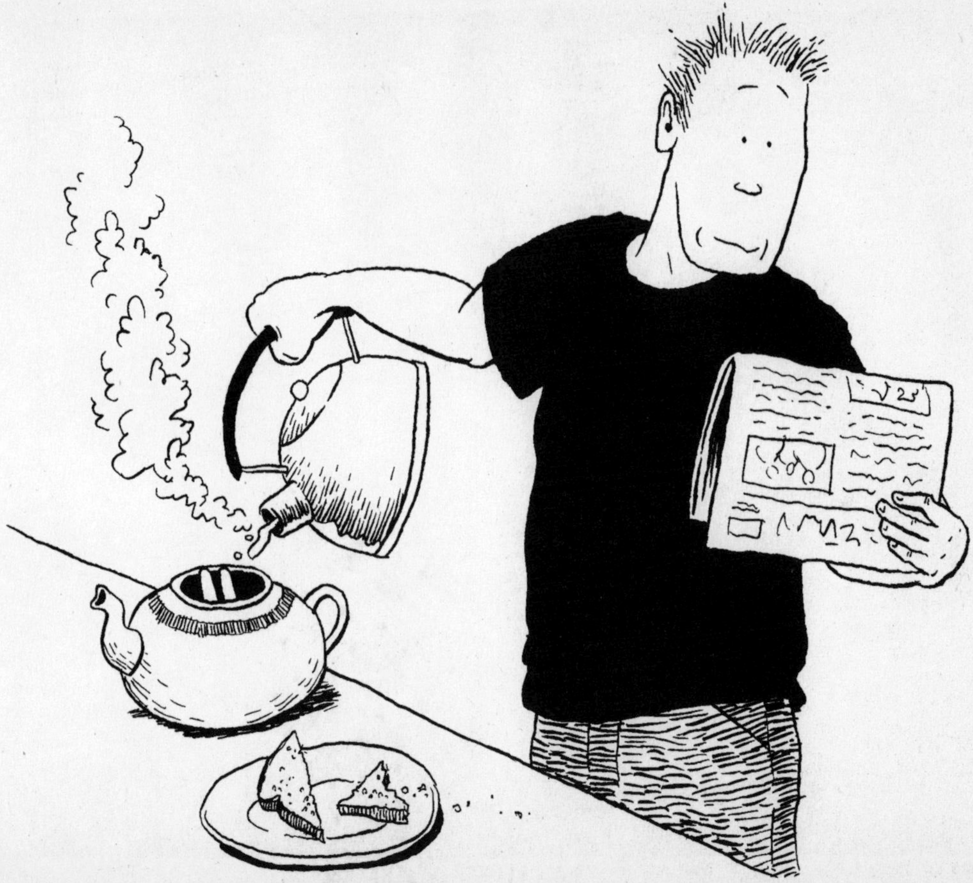

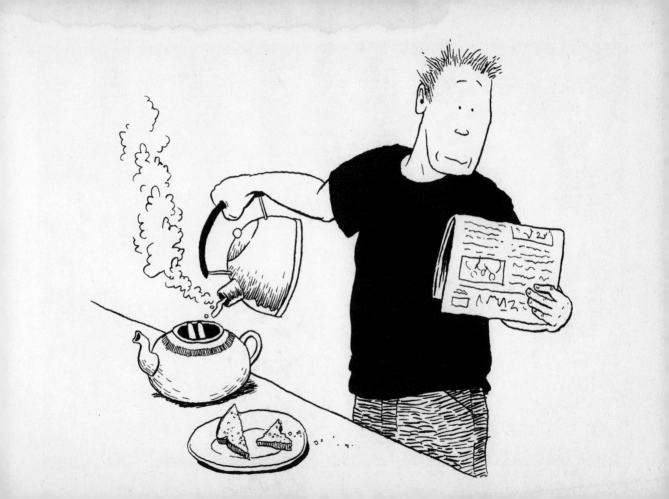

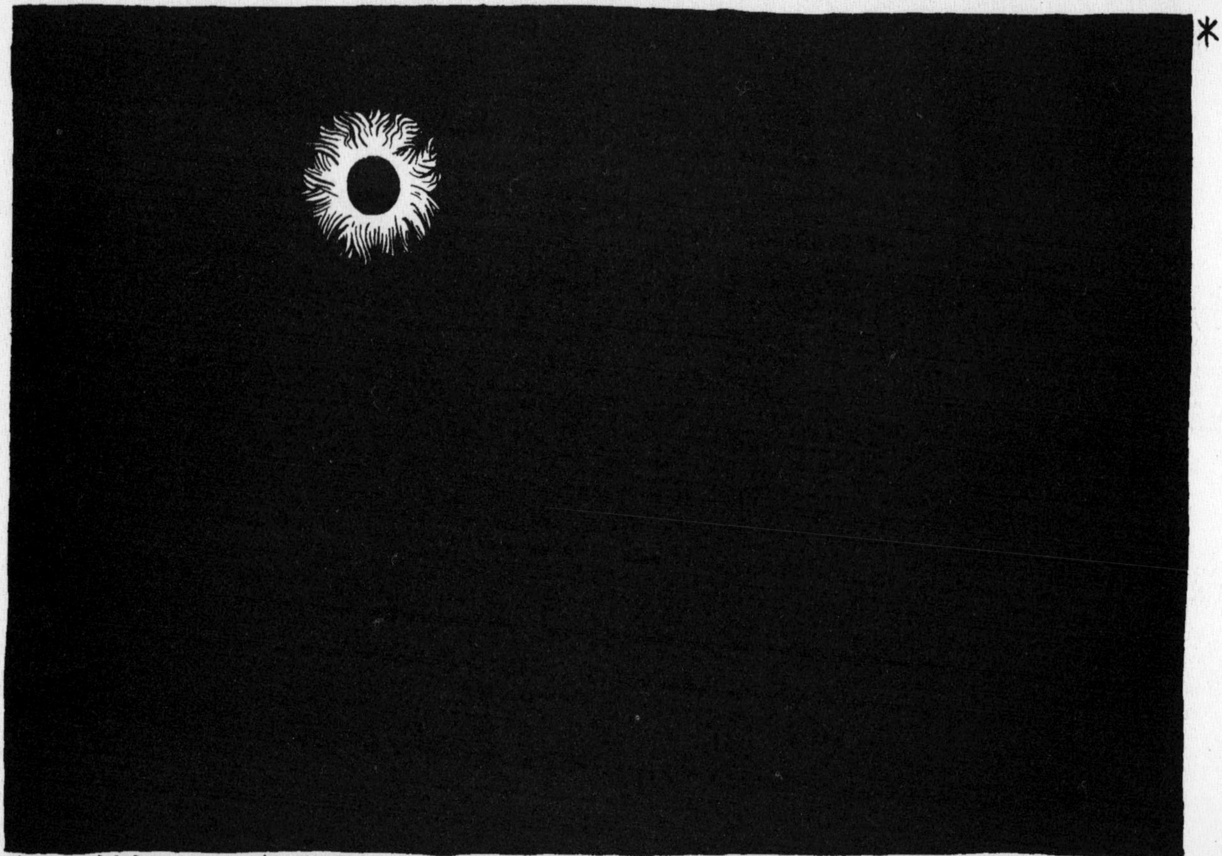
*

* TWO RABBITS JUGGLING CHISELS DURING A TOTAL ECLIPSE OF THE SUN

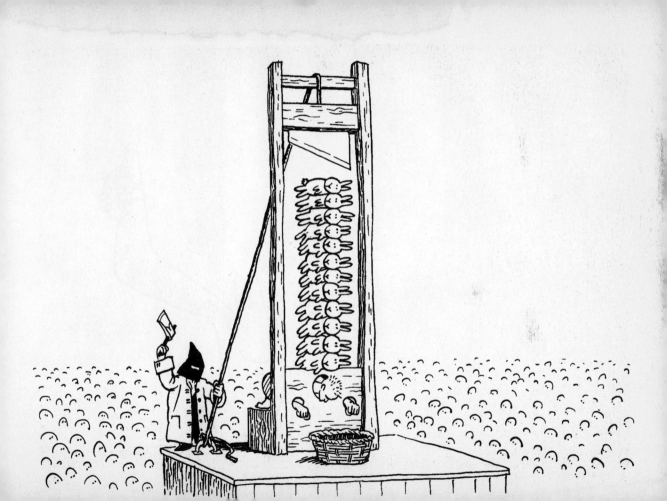

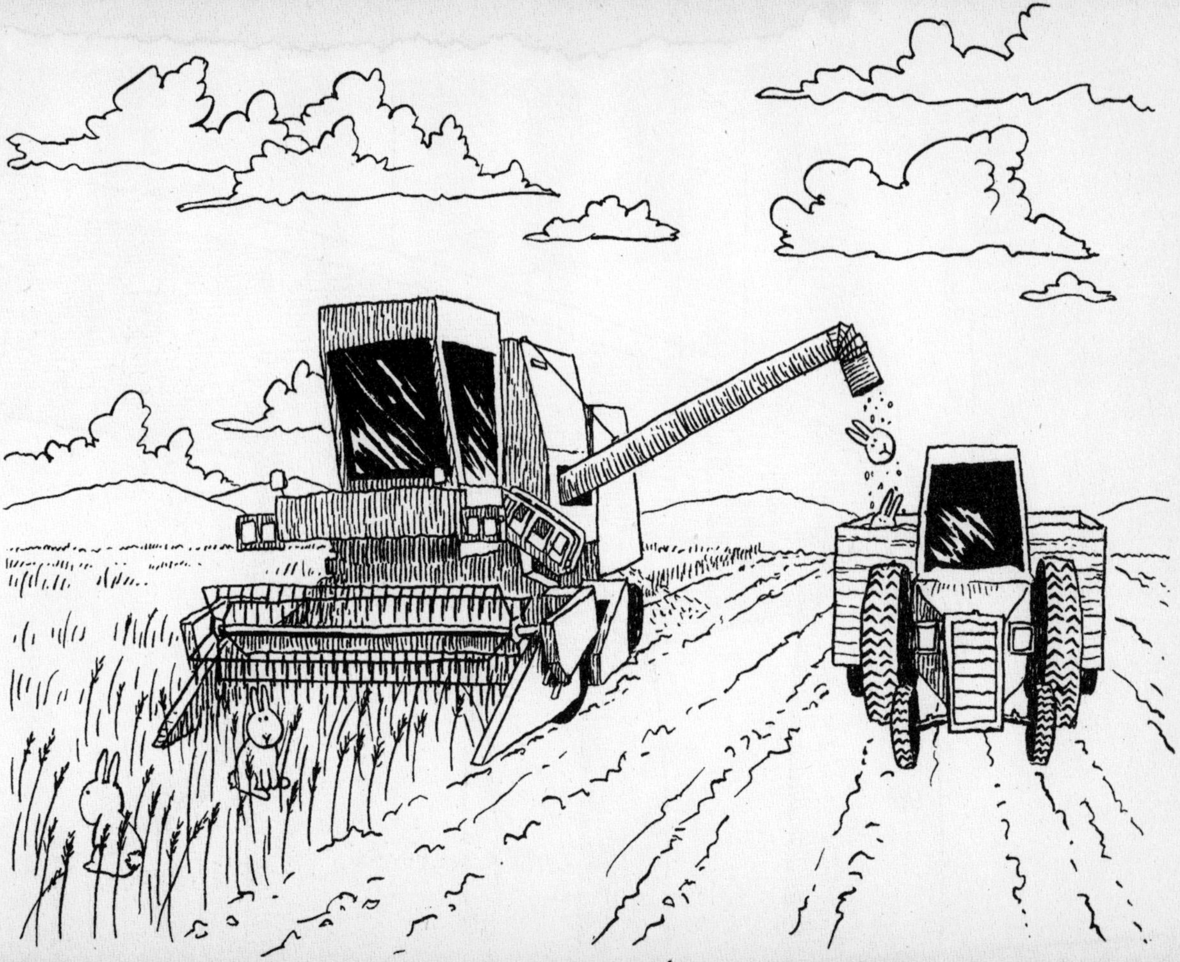

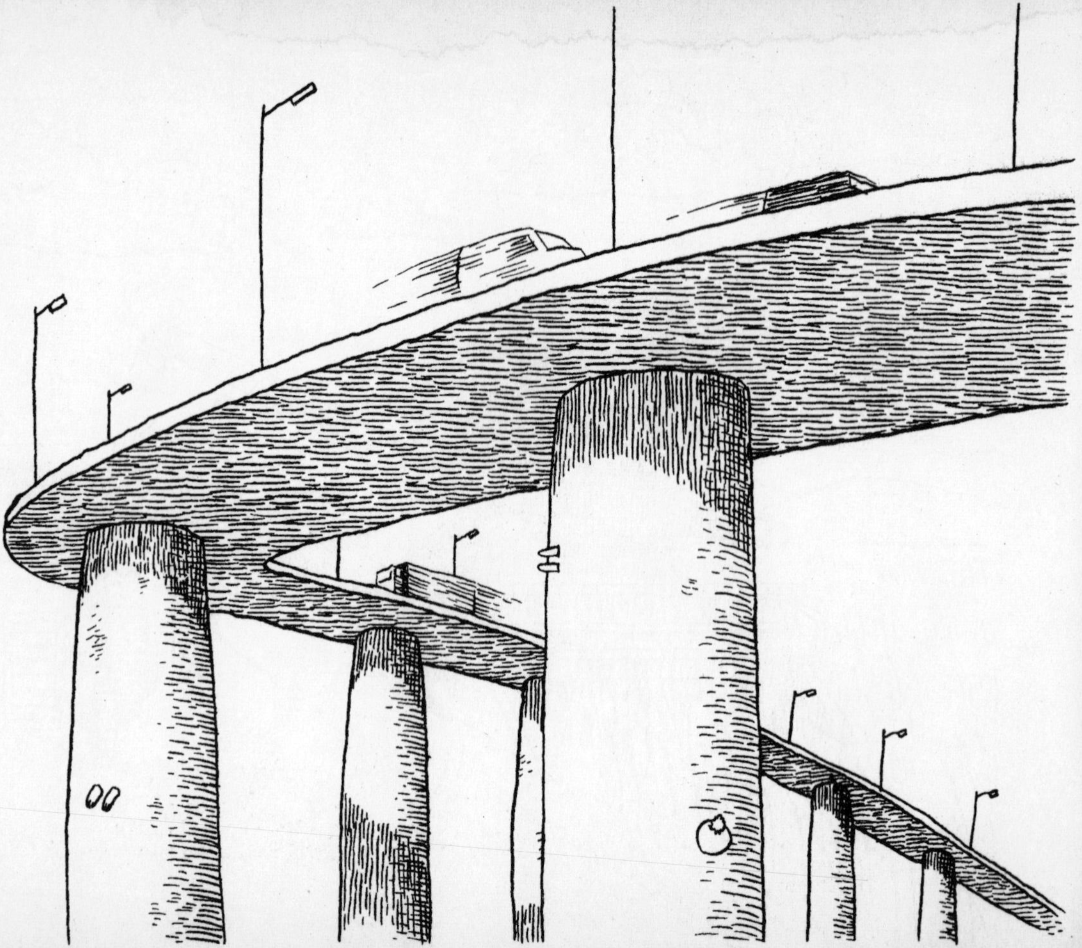

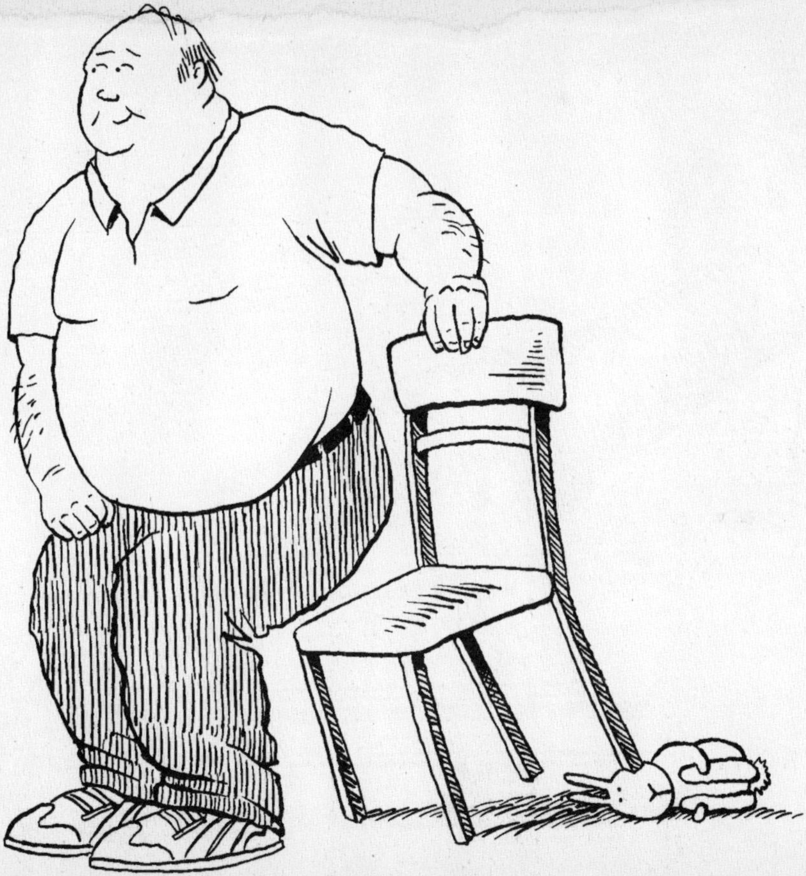

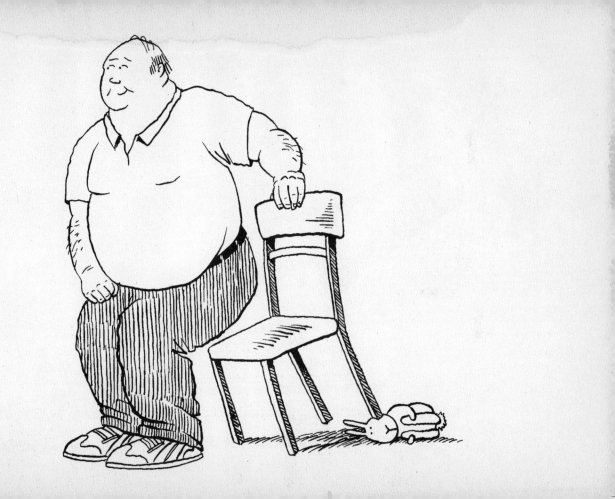

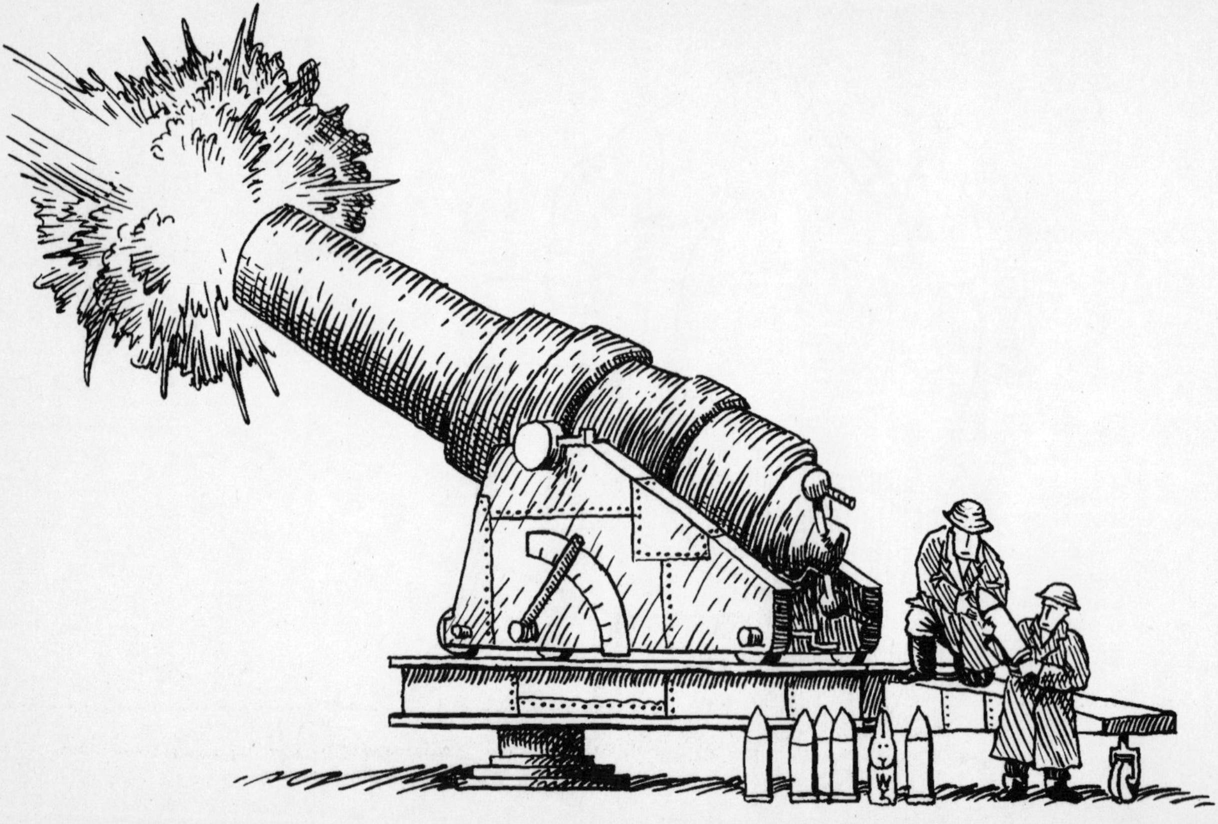

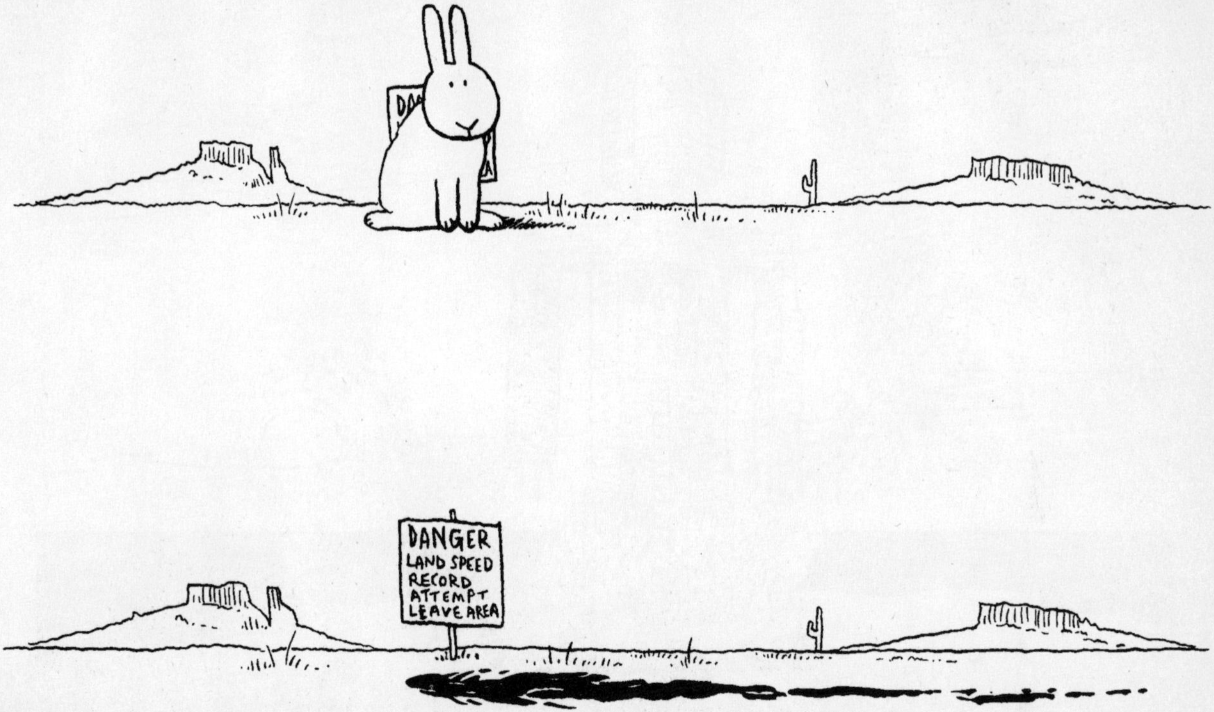
DANGER
LAND SPEED
RECORD
ATTEMPT
LEAVE AREA

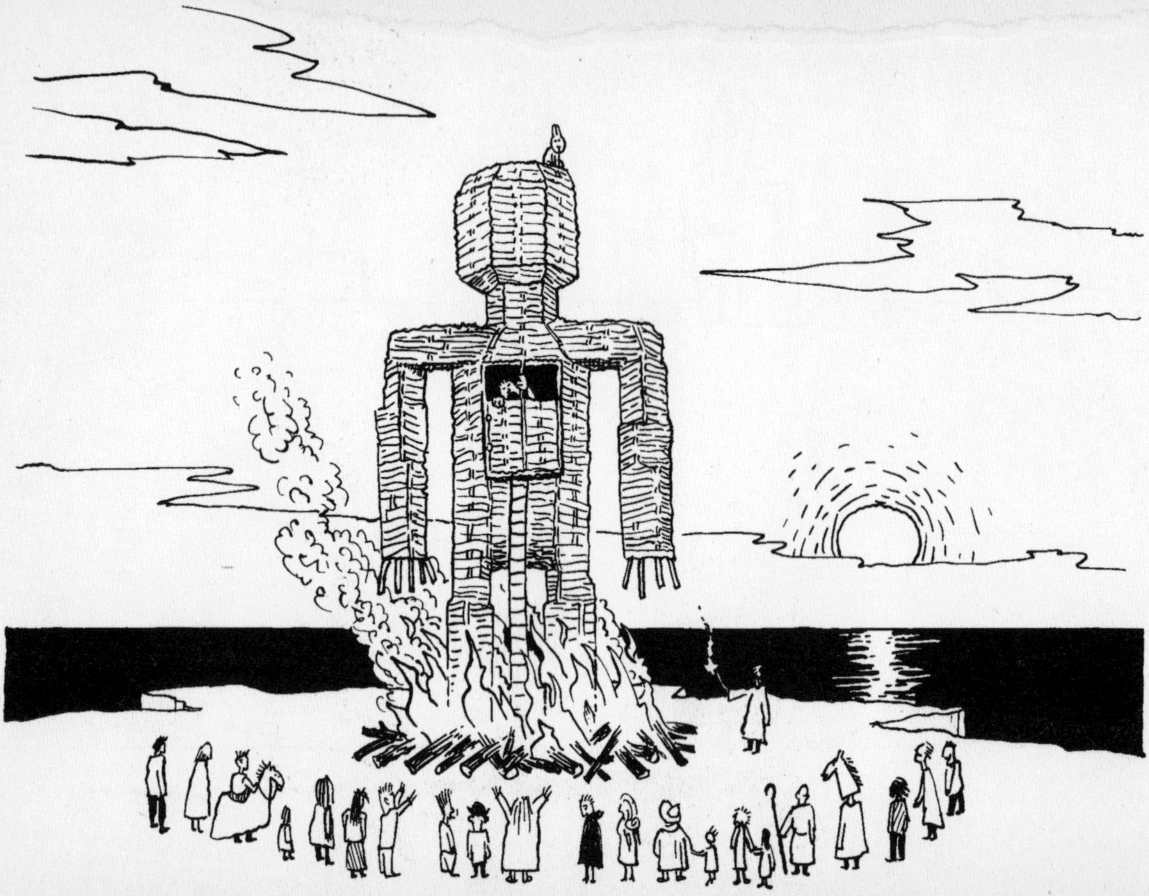

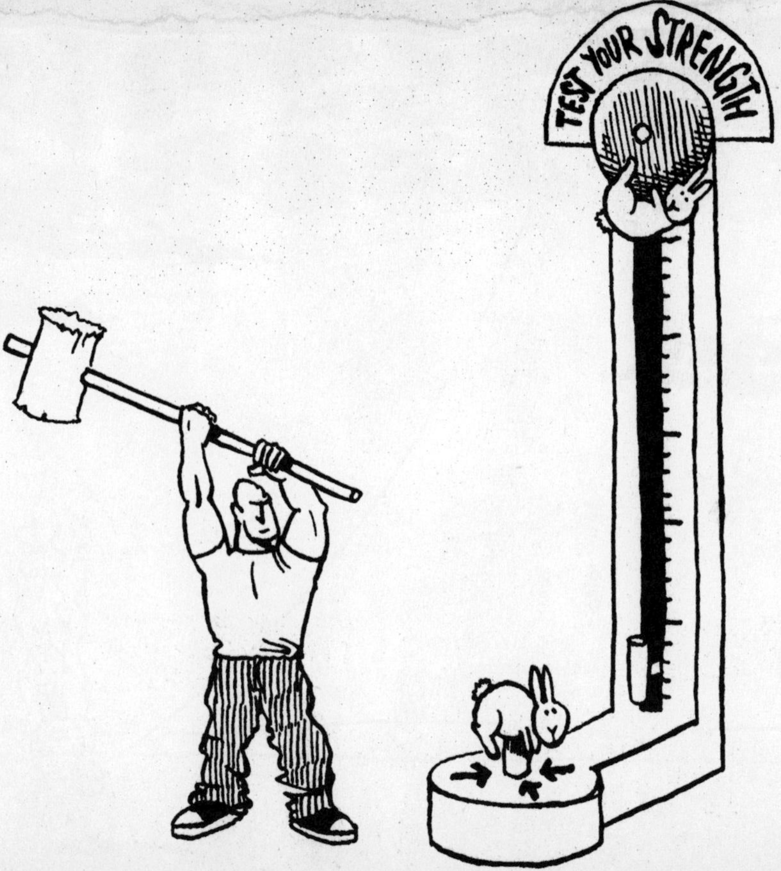
TEST YOUR STRENGTH

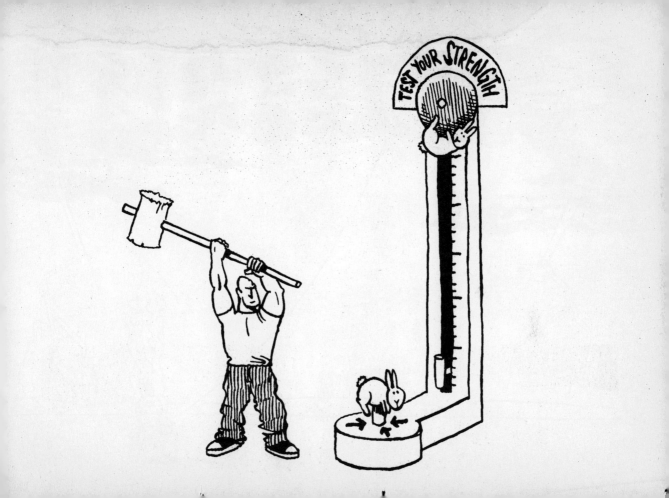

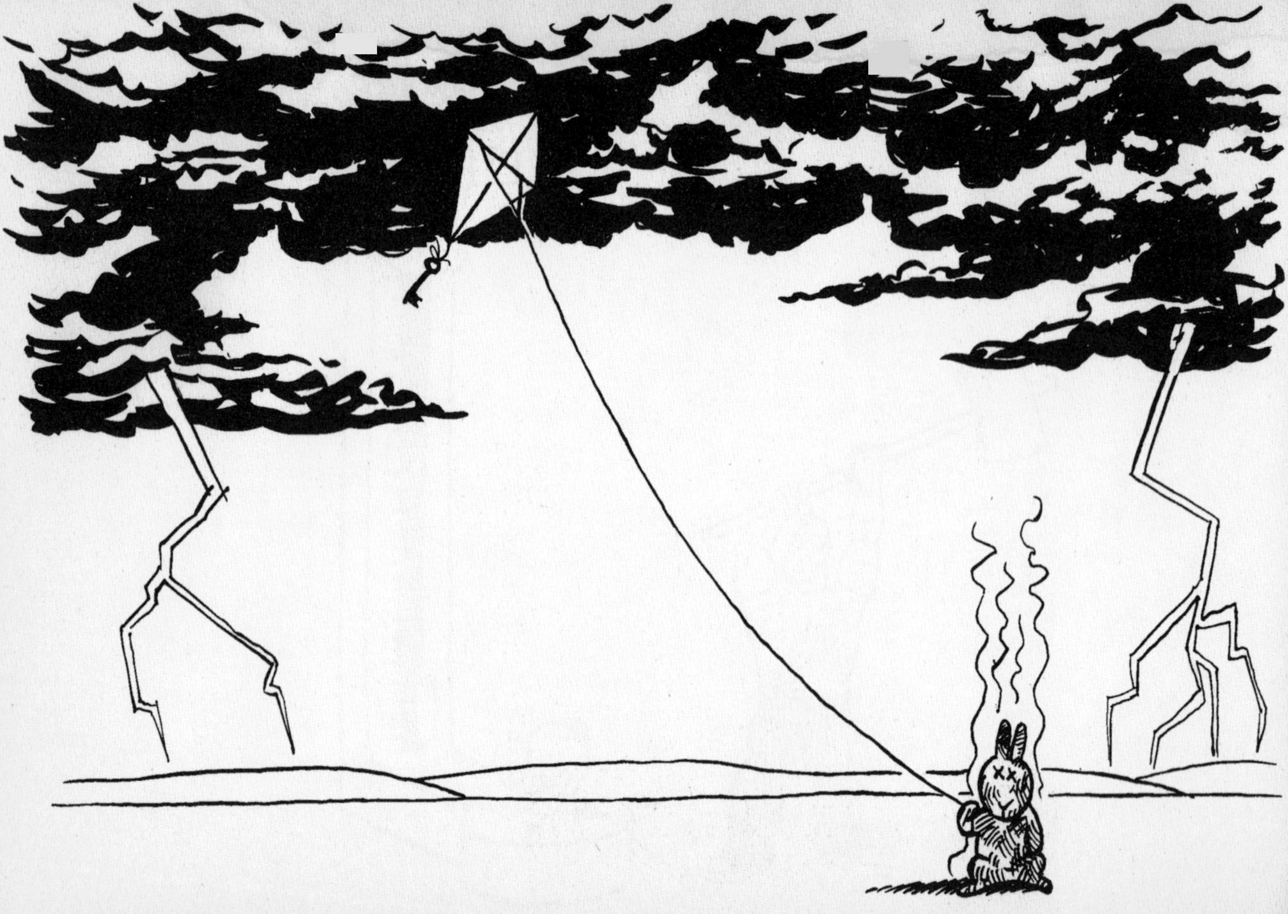

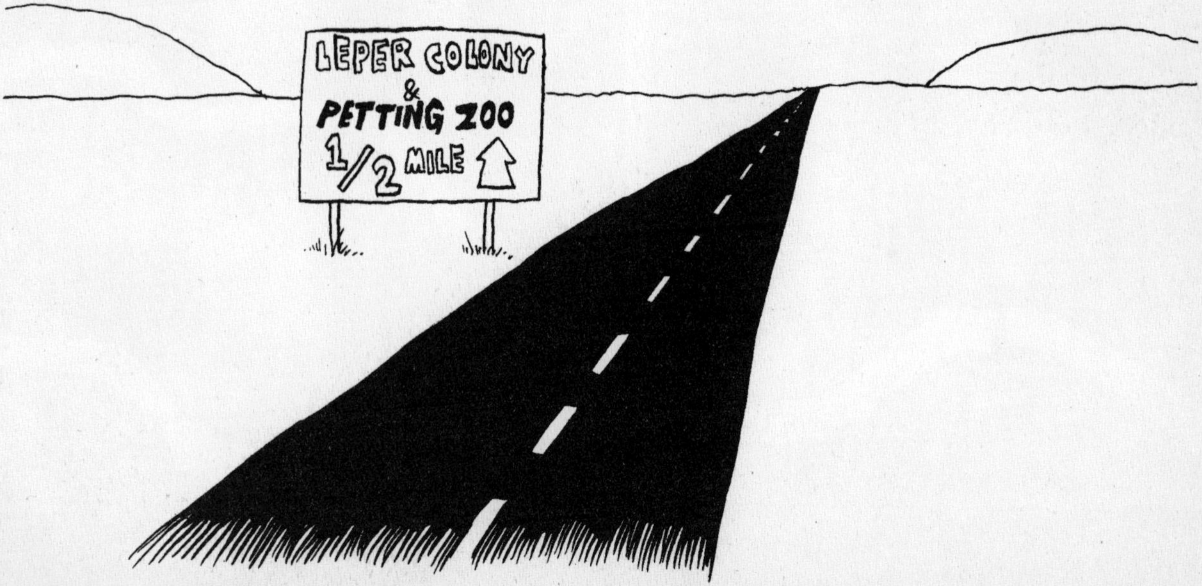
LEPER COLONY
&
PETTING ZOO
1/2 MILE

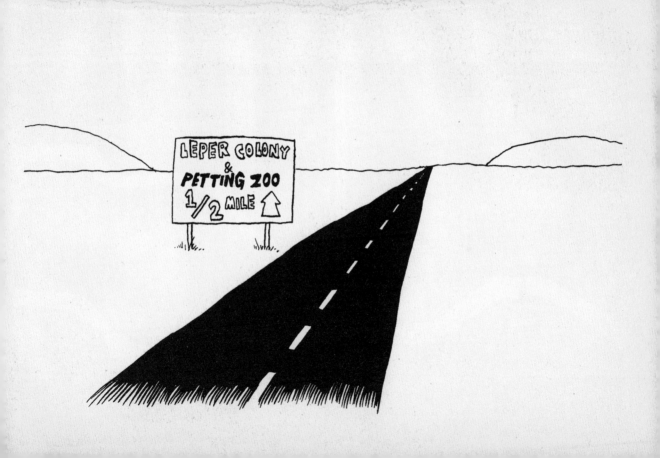

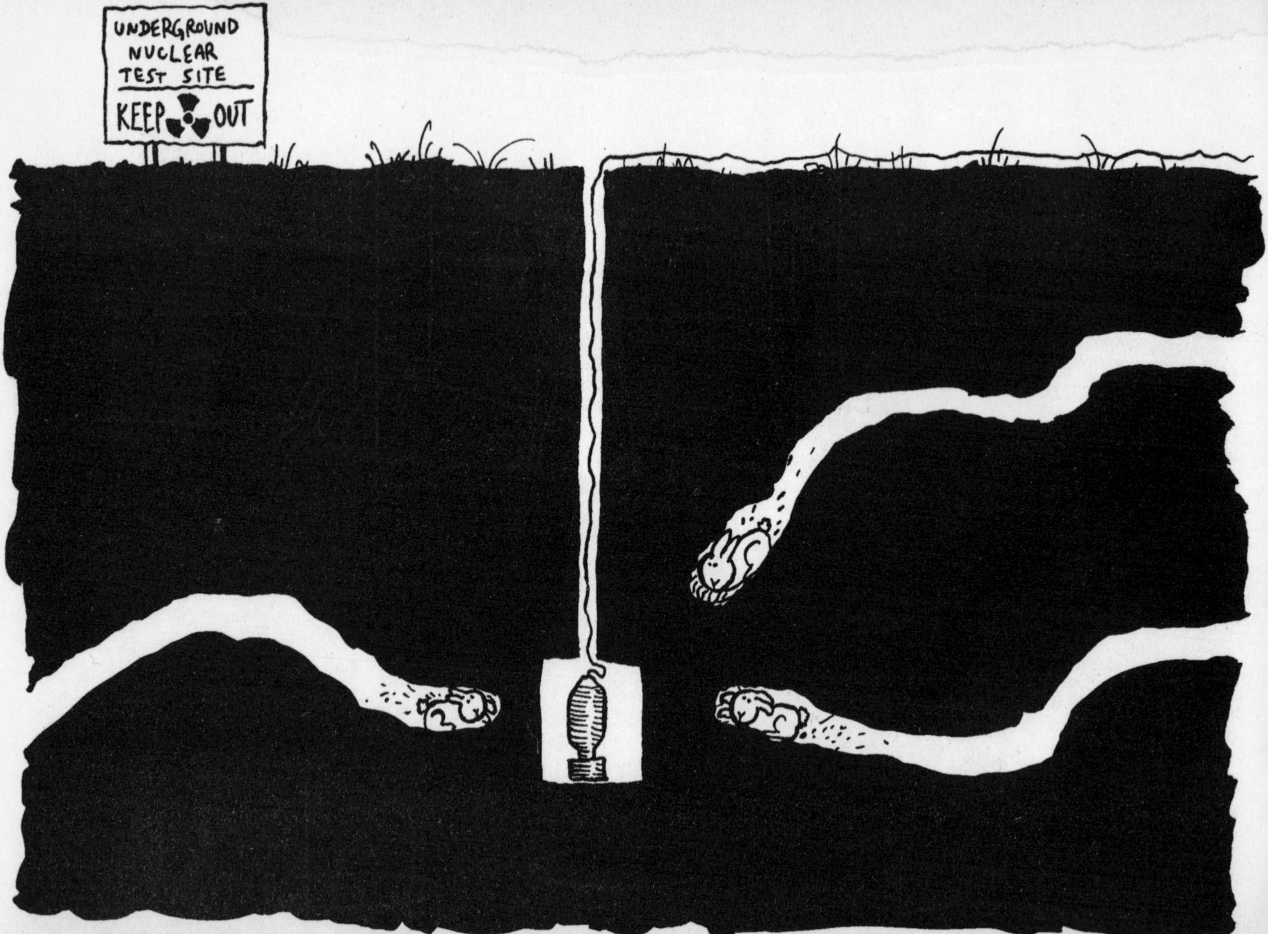
UNDERGROUND
NUCLEAR
TEST SITE
KEEP OUT

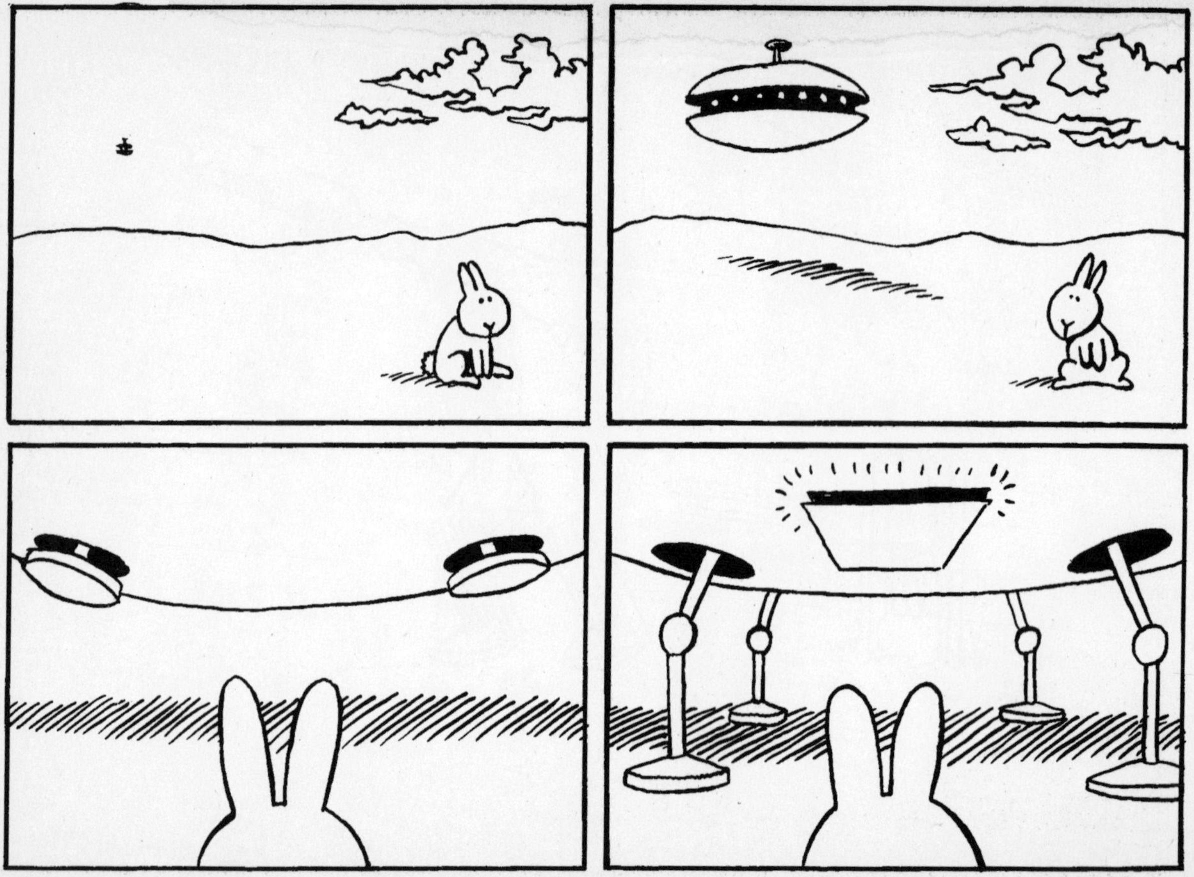

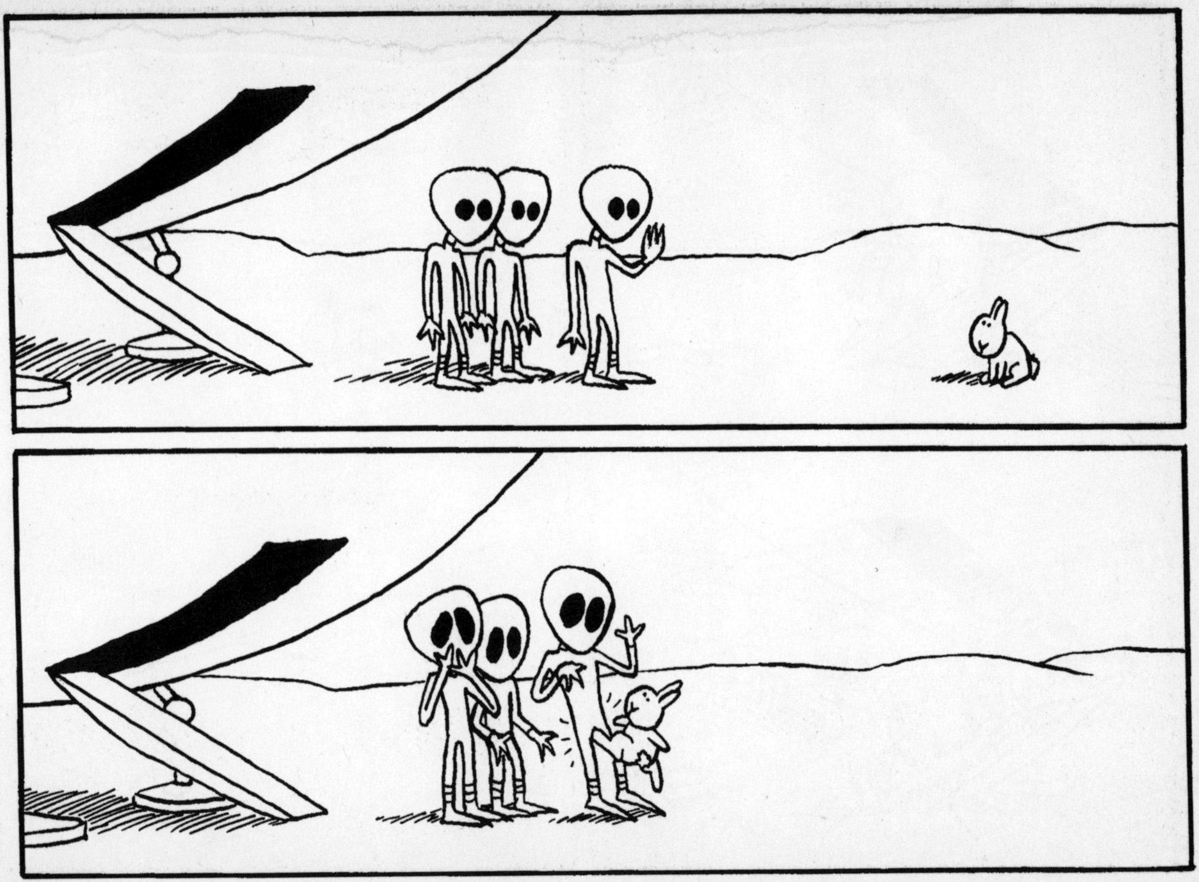

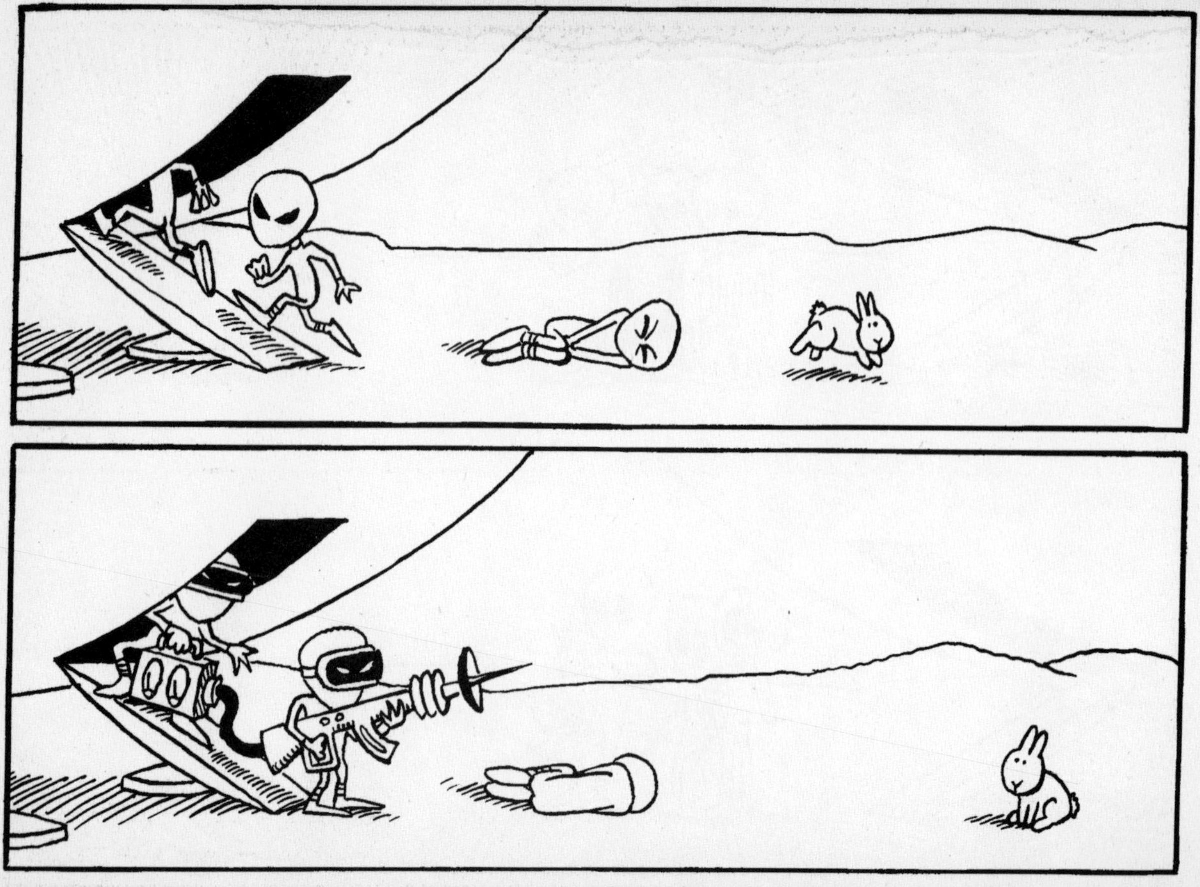

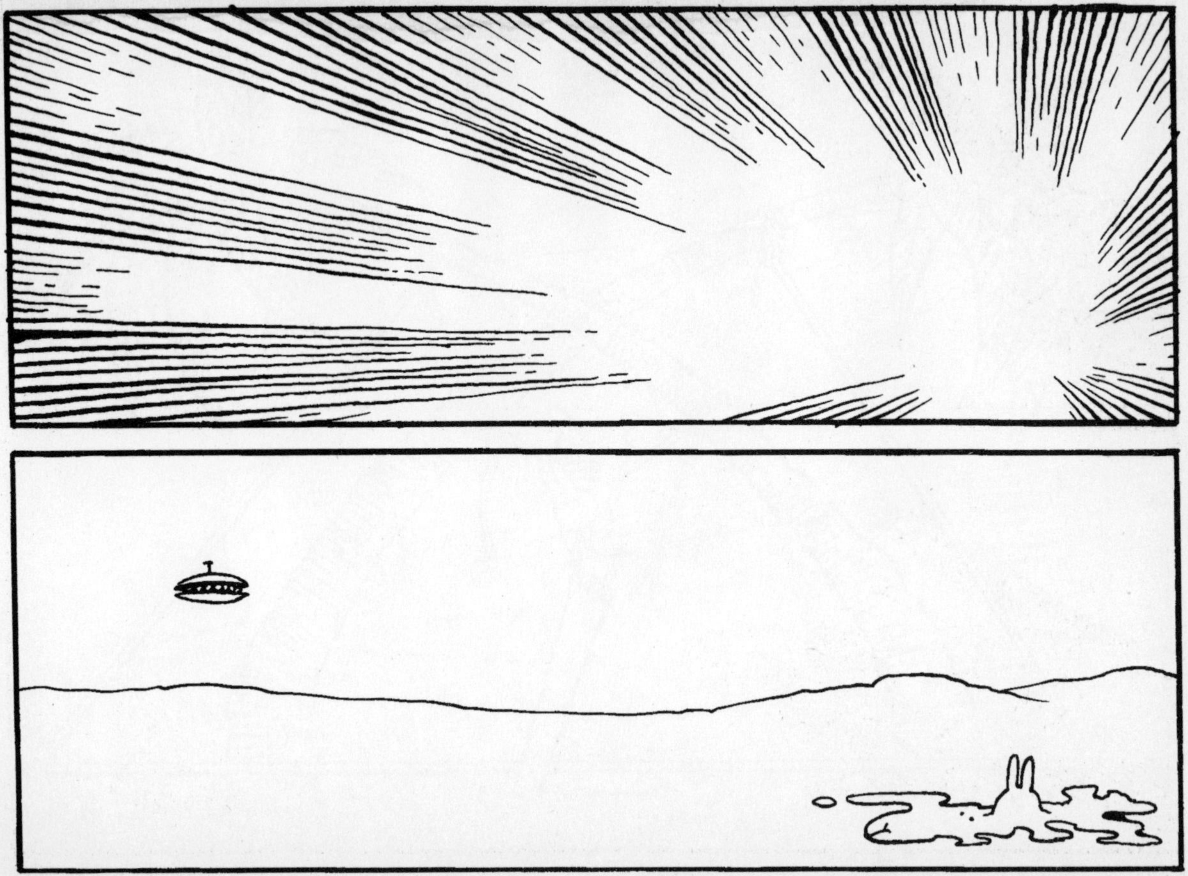

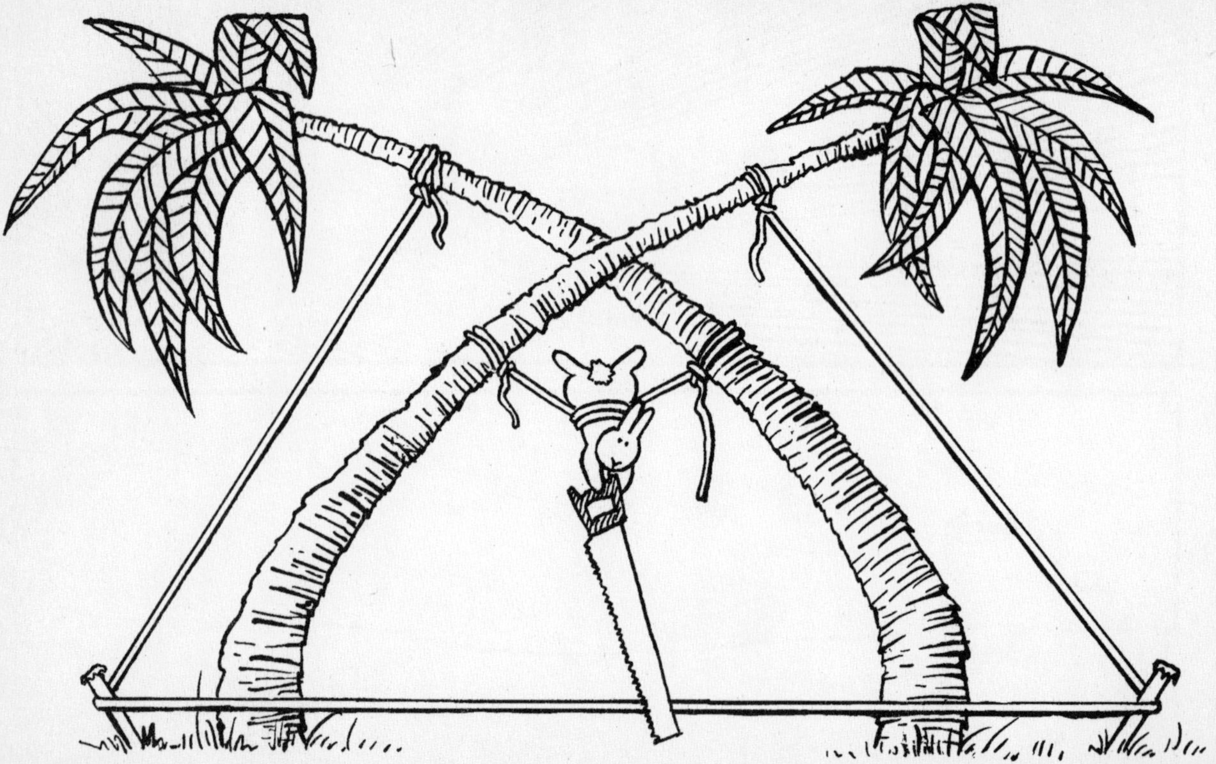

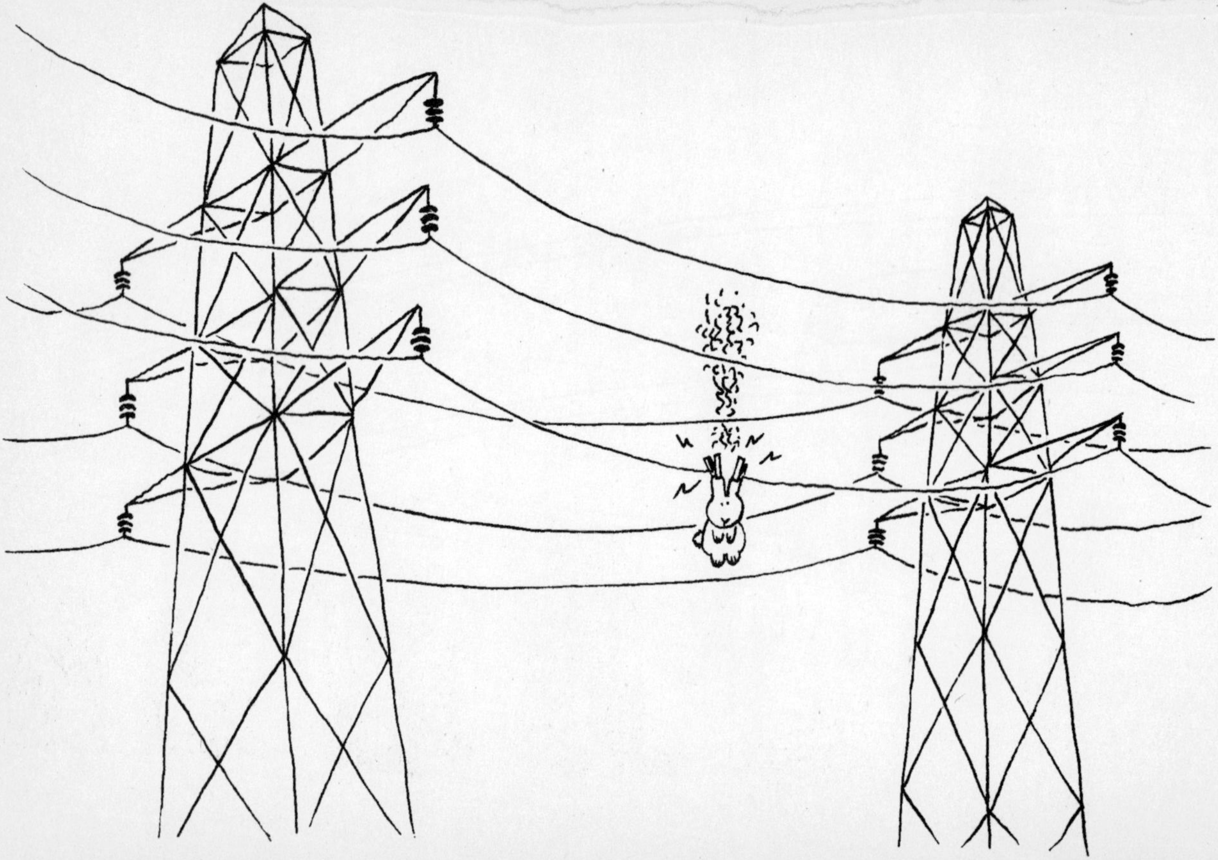

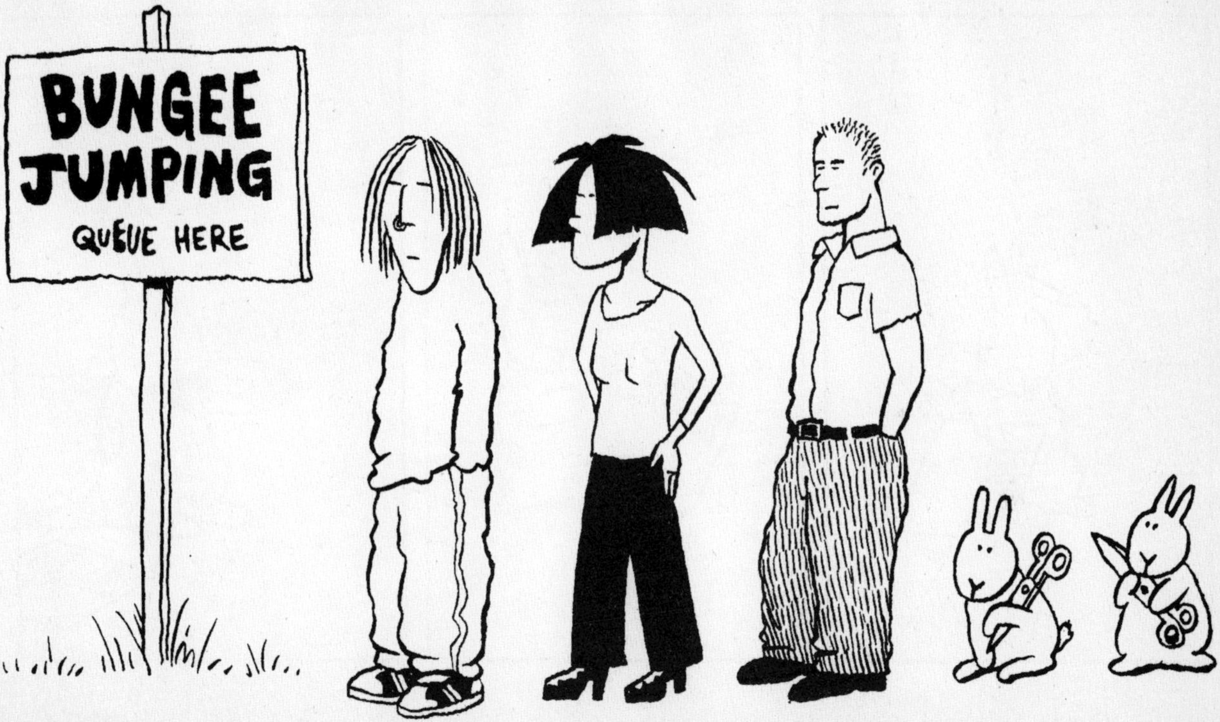
BUNGEE JUMPING
QUEUE HERE

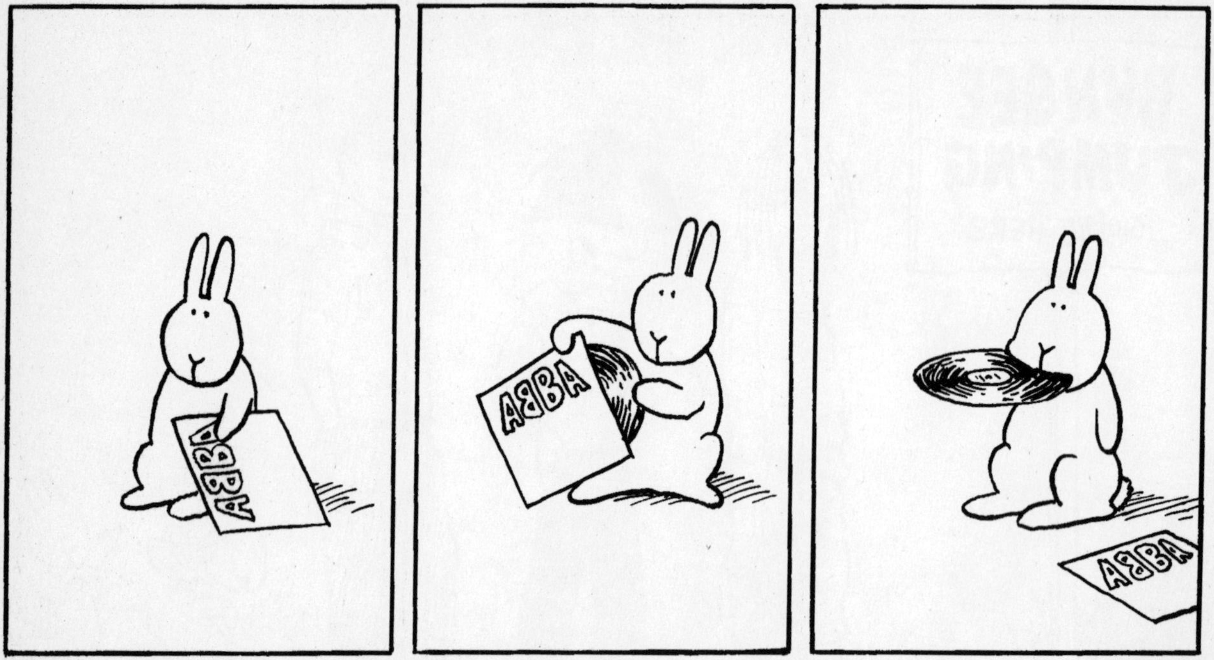
ABBA
ABBA
ABBA

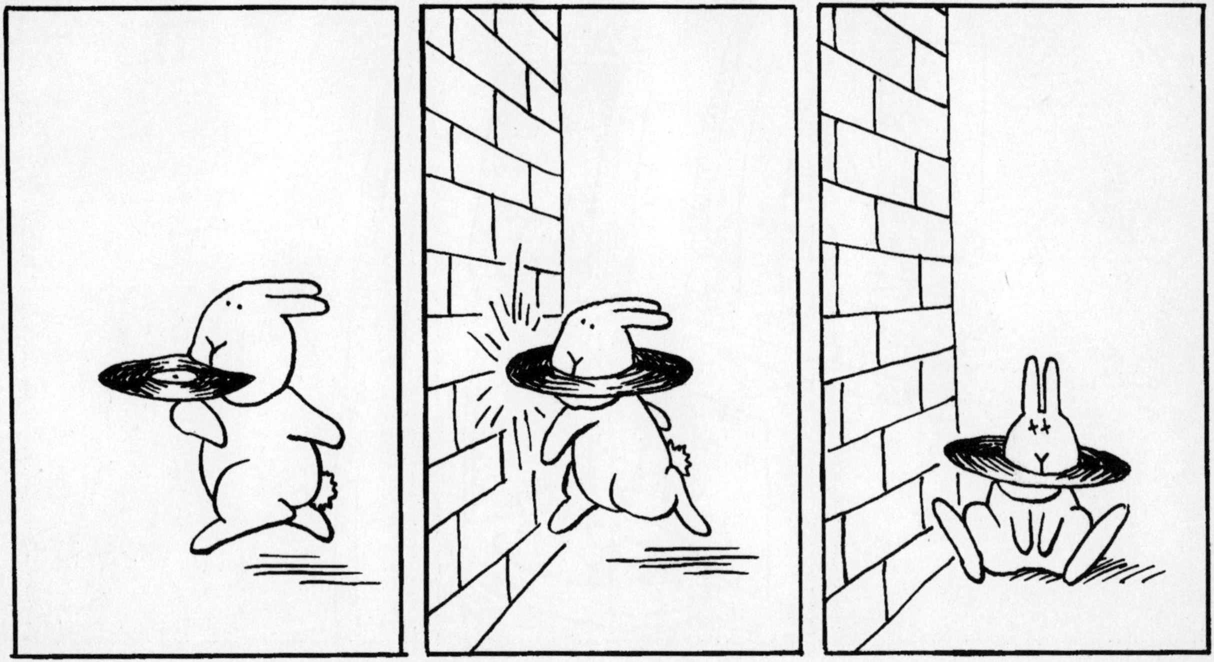

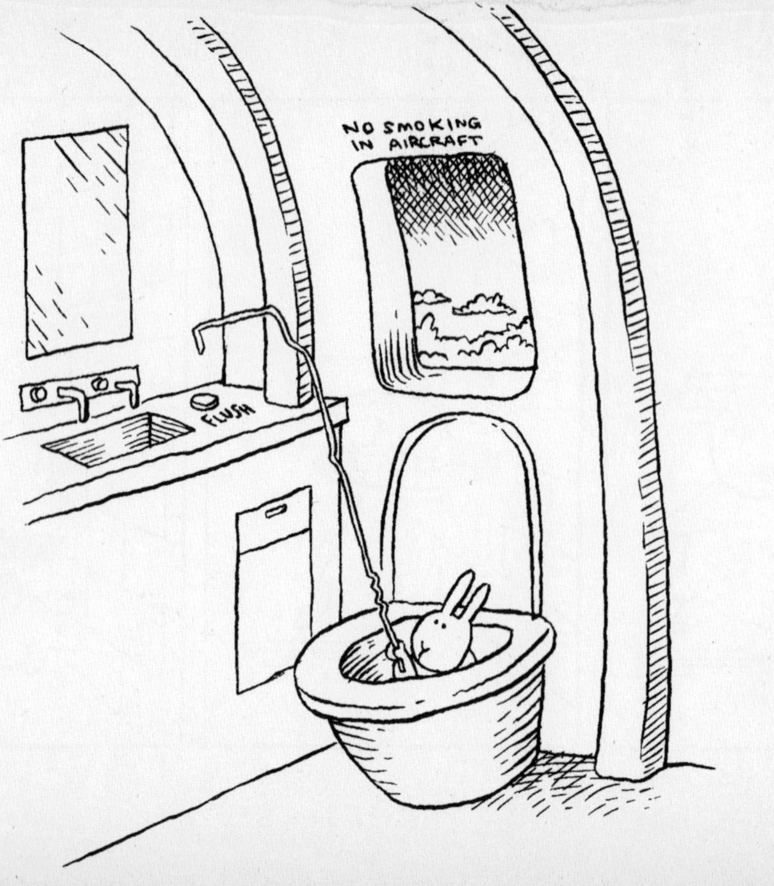
NO SMOKING IN AIRCRAFT
FLUSH

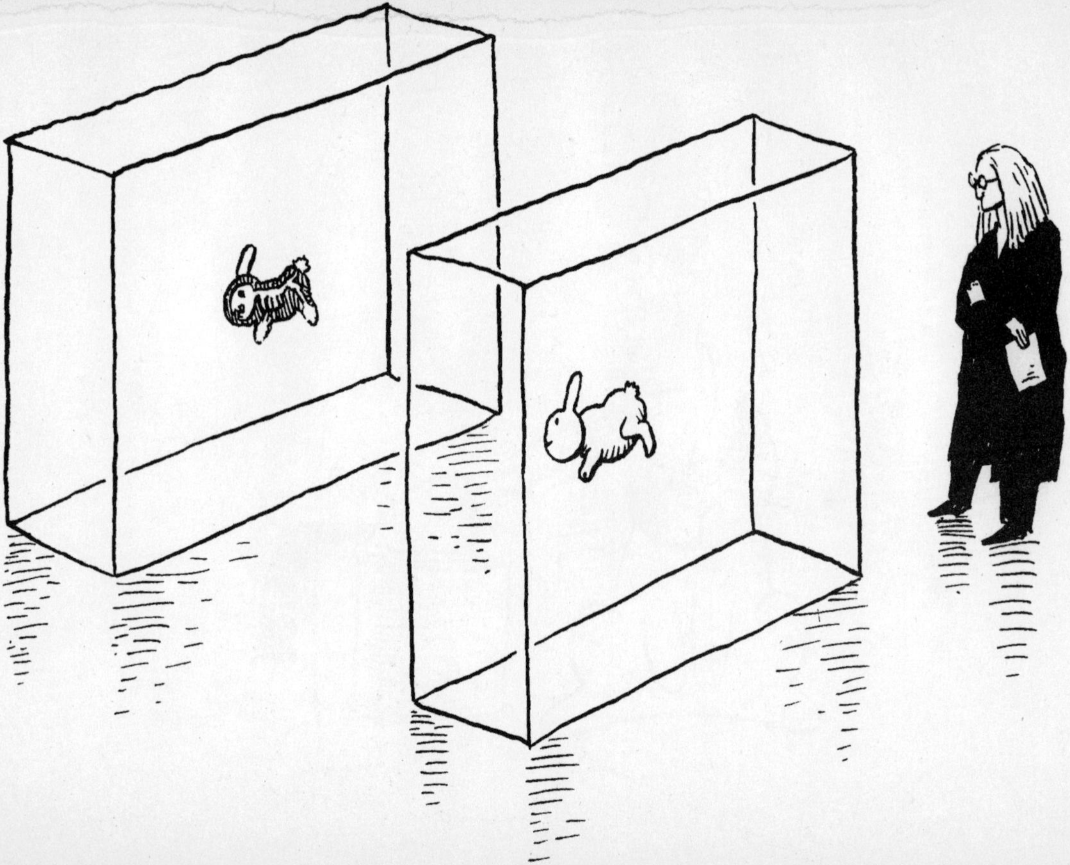

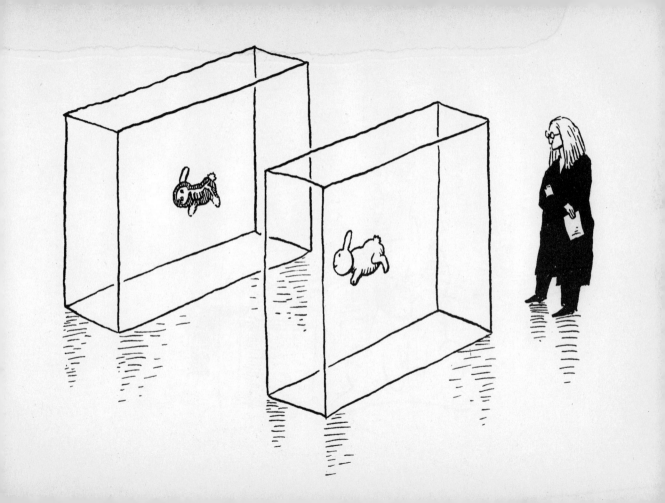

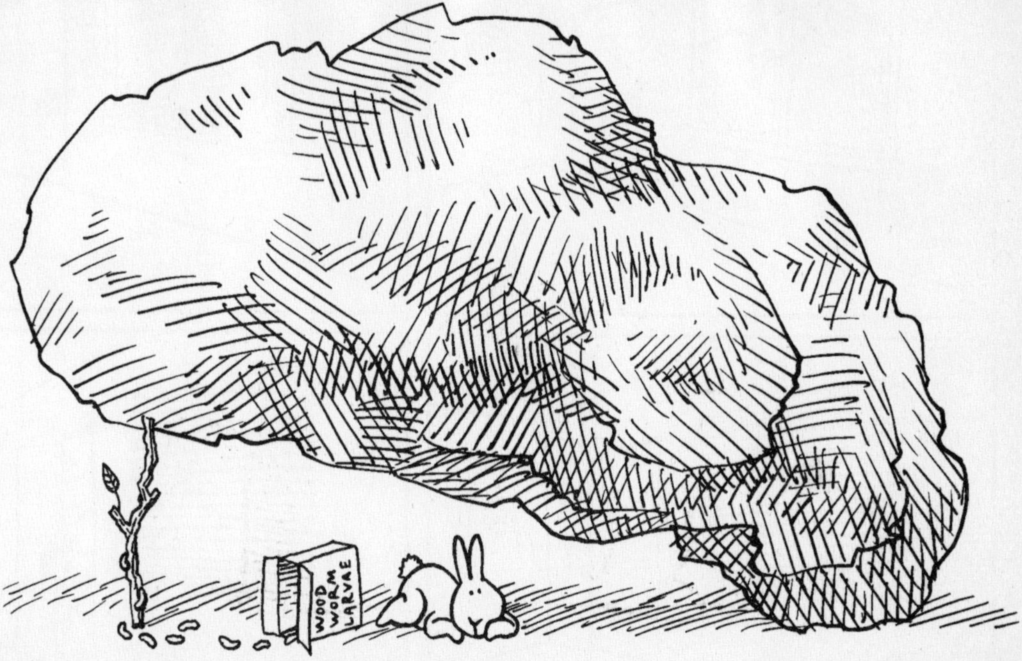
WOOD
WORM
LARVAE

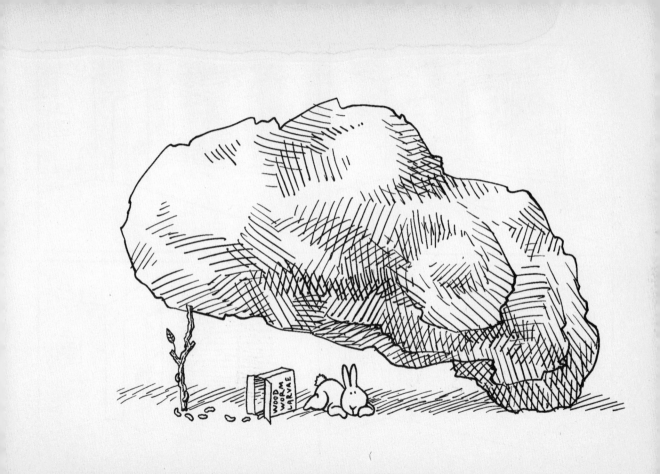

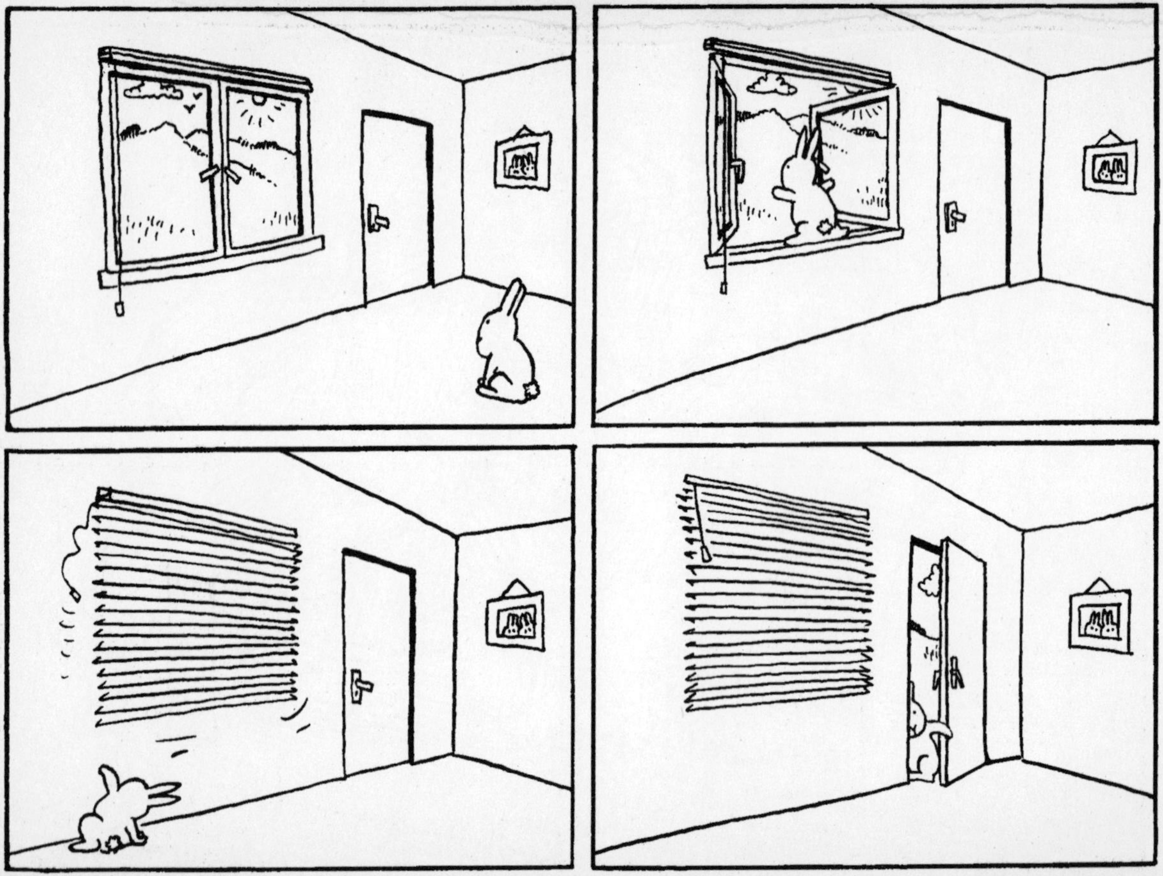

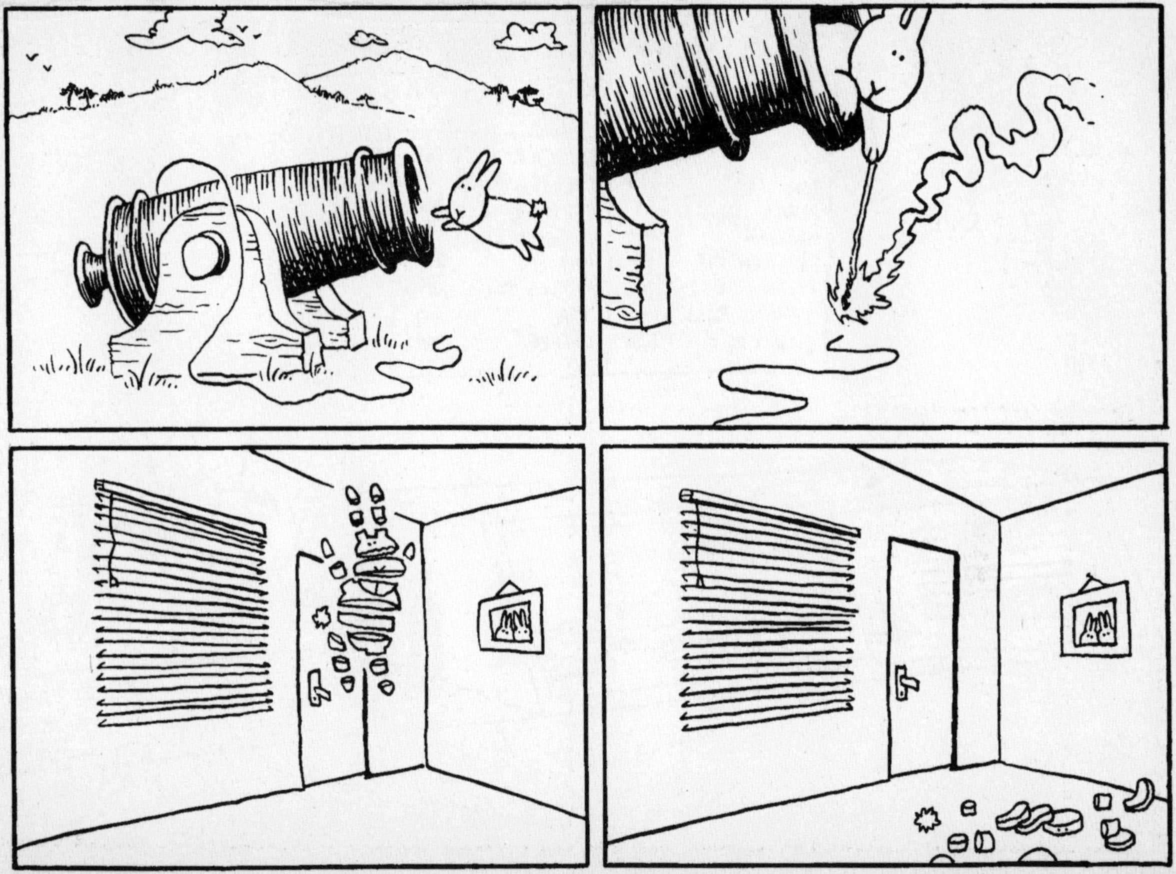

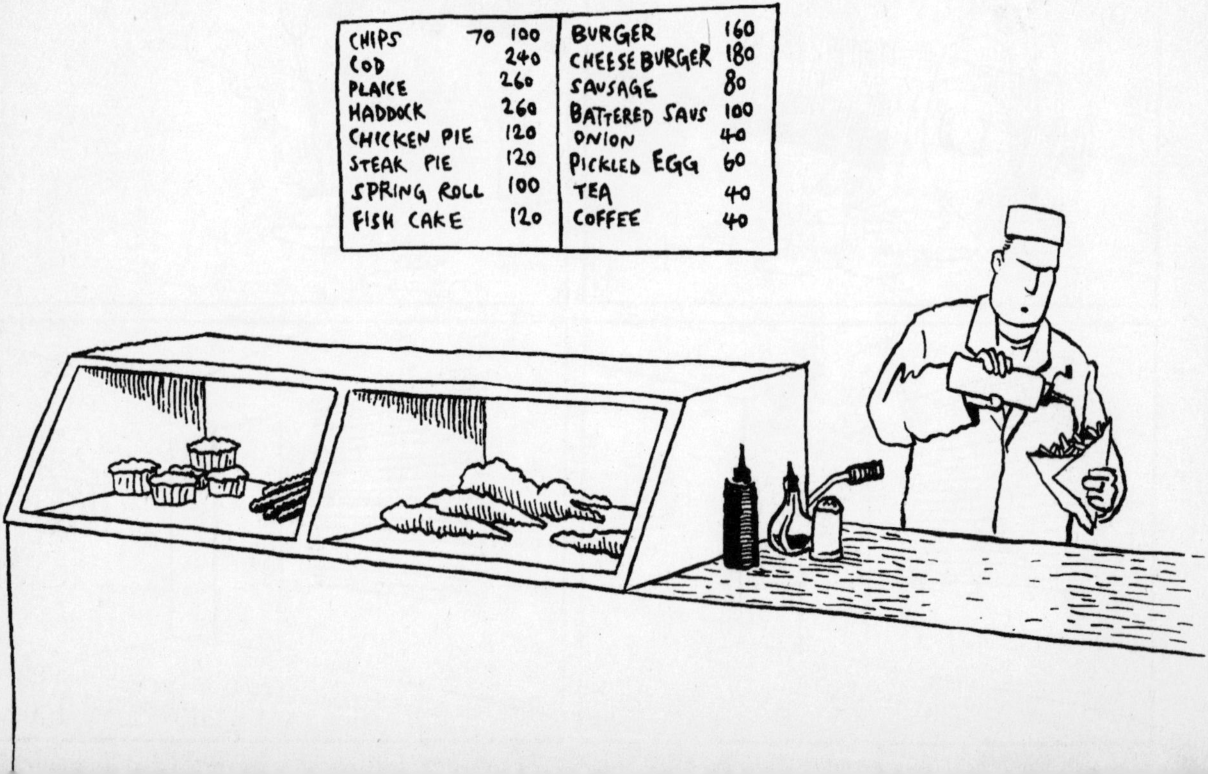
CHIPS 70 100
COD 240
PLAICE 260
HADDOCK 260
CHICKEN PIE 120
STEAK PIE 120
SPRING ROLL 100
FISH CAKE 120
BURGER 160
CHEESEBURGER 180
SAUSAGE 80
BATTERED SAUS 100
ONION 40
PICKLED EGG 60
TEA 40
COFFEE 40

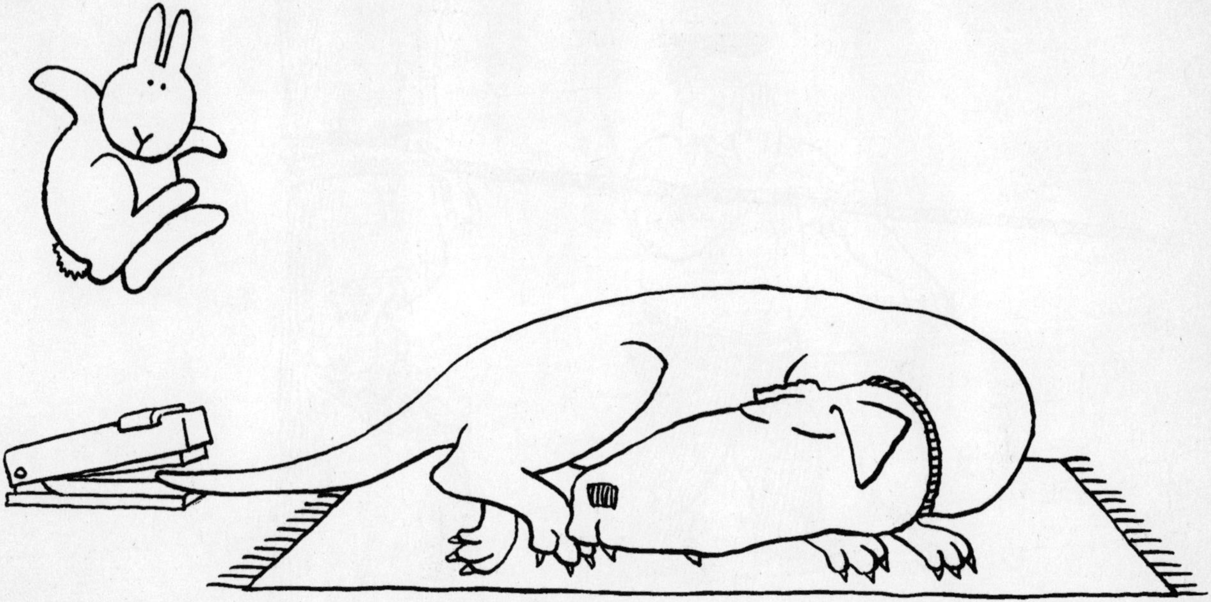

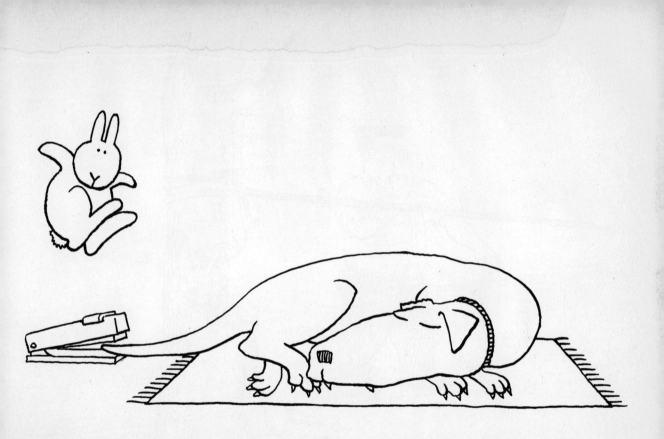

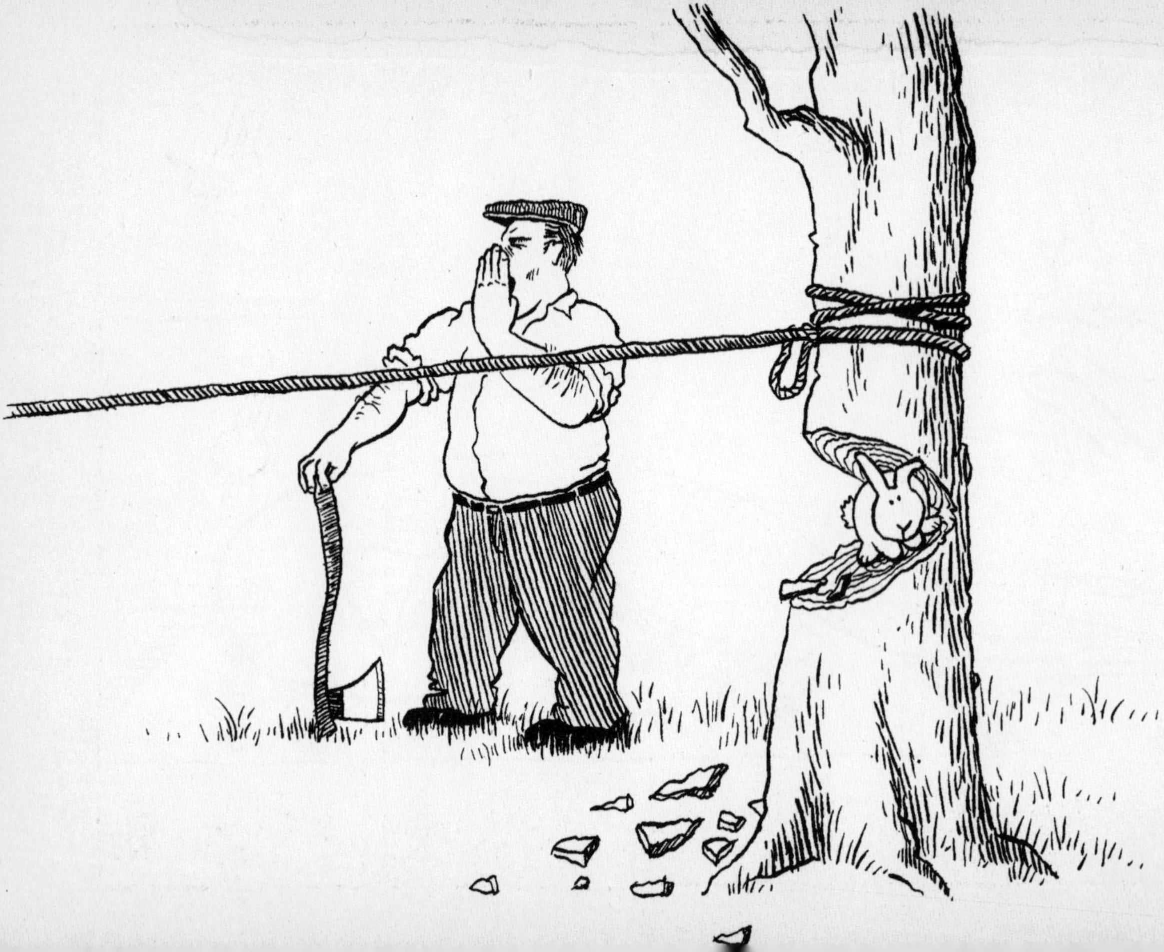

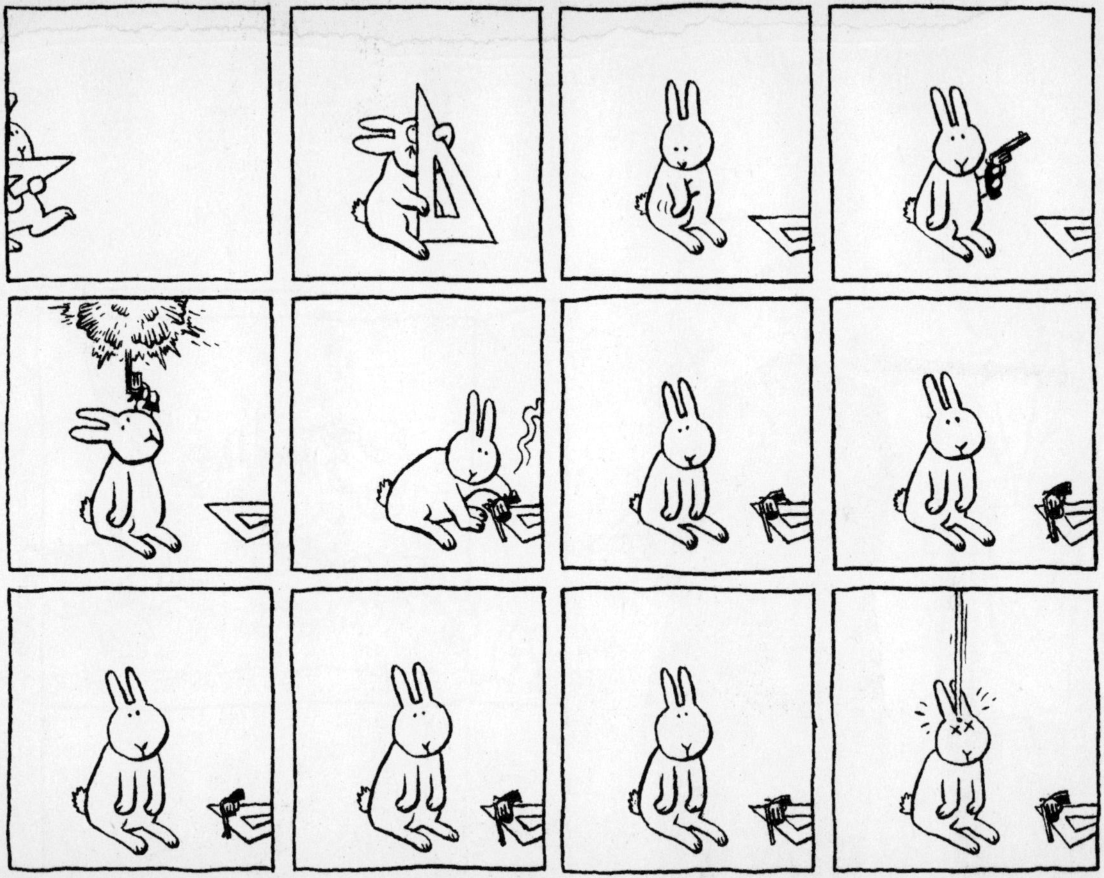

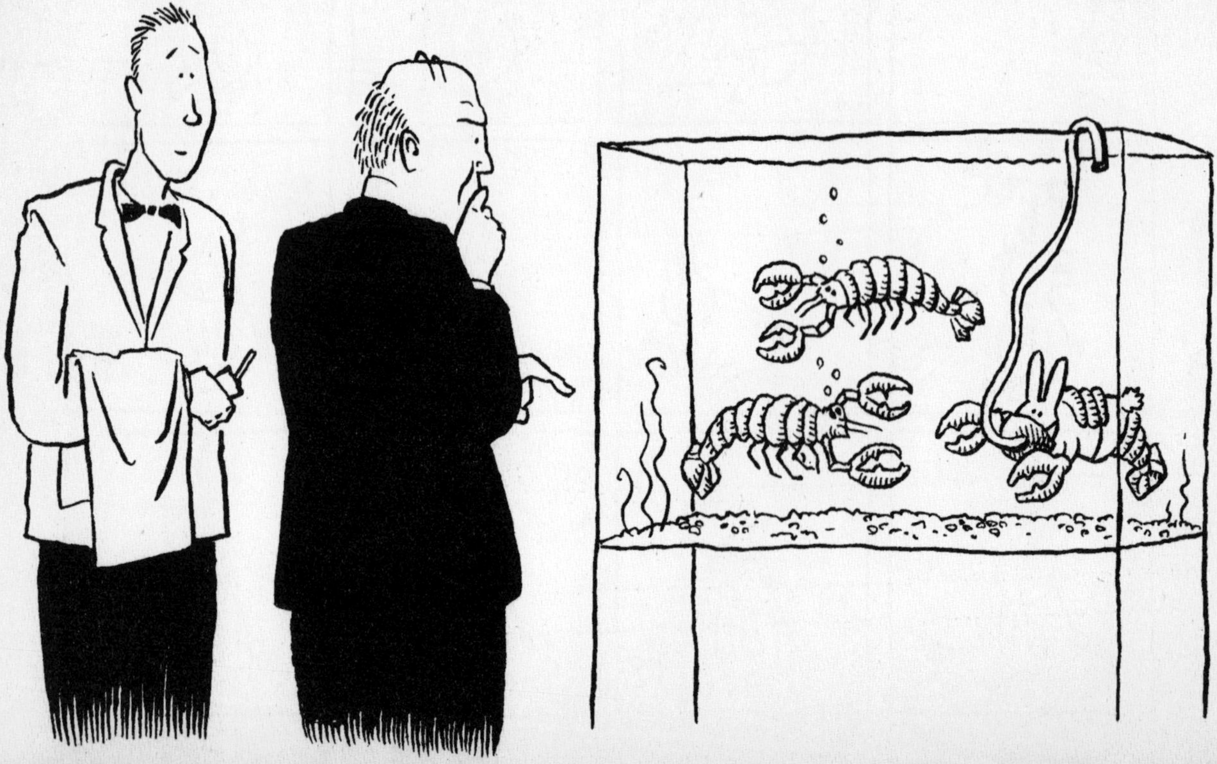

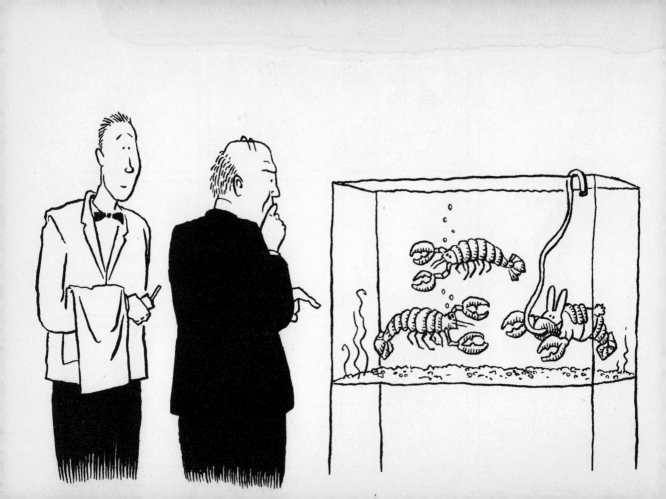

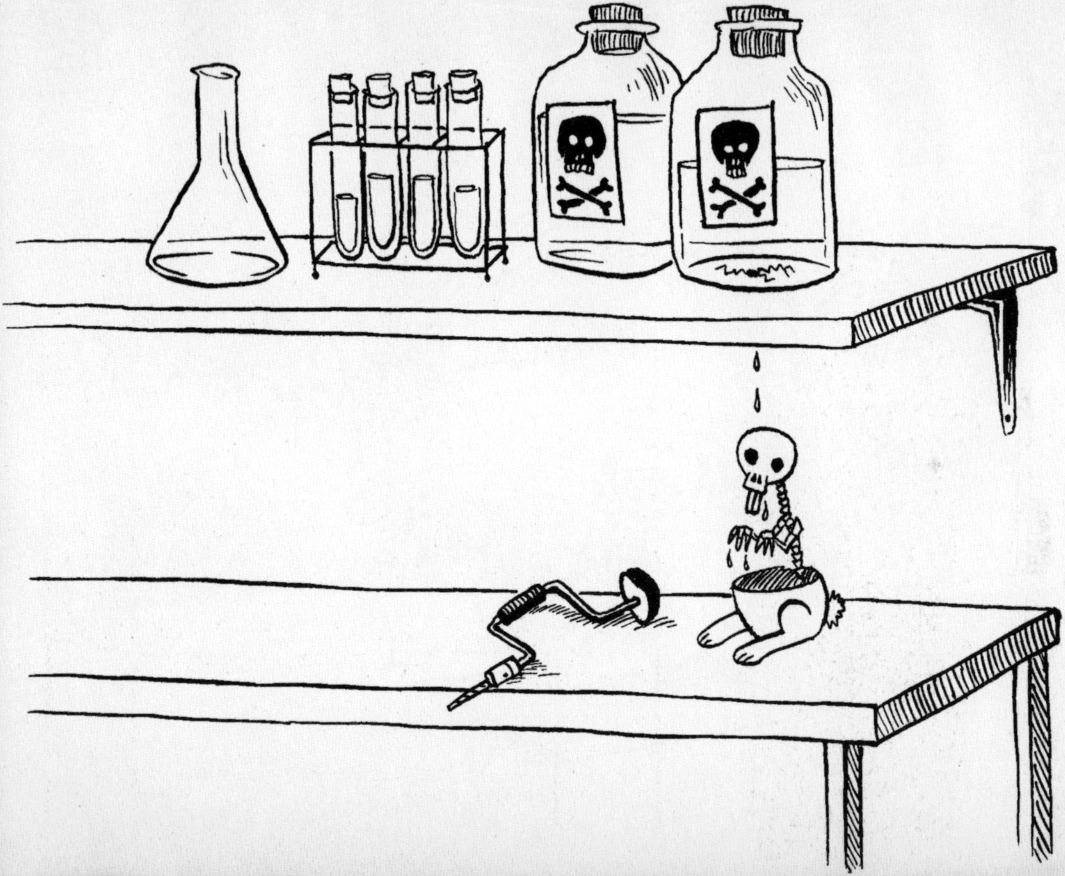

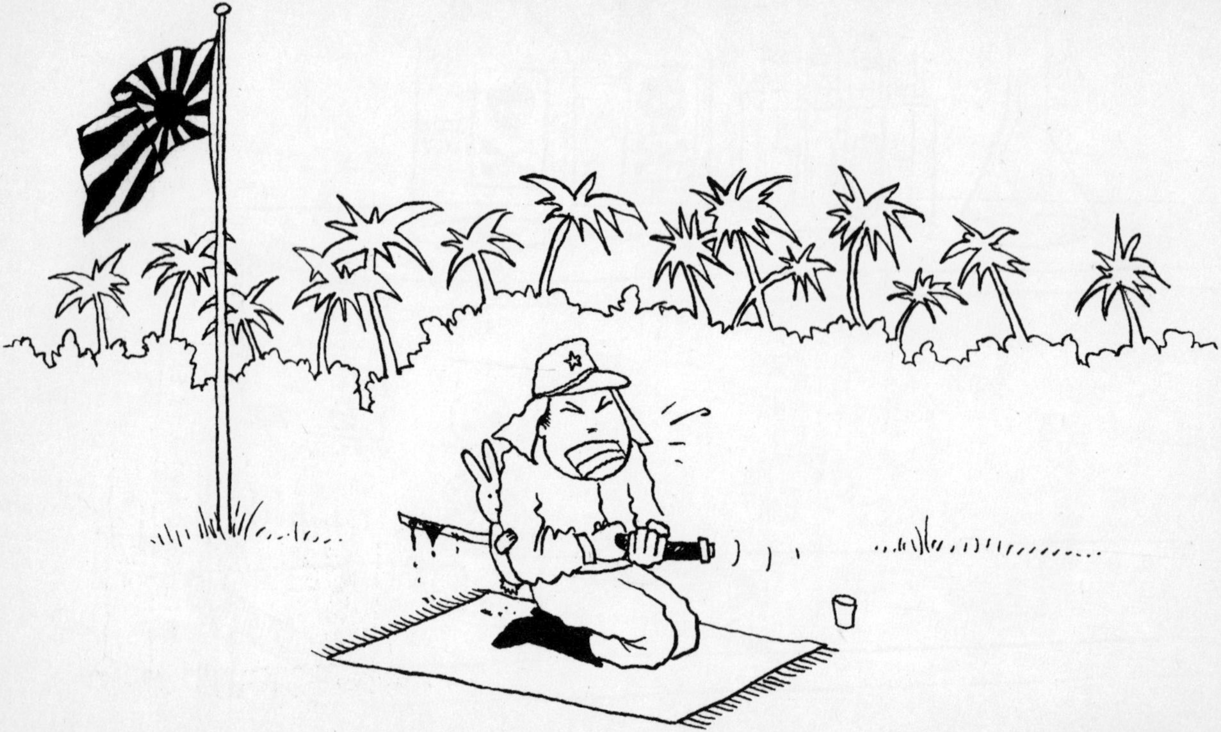

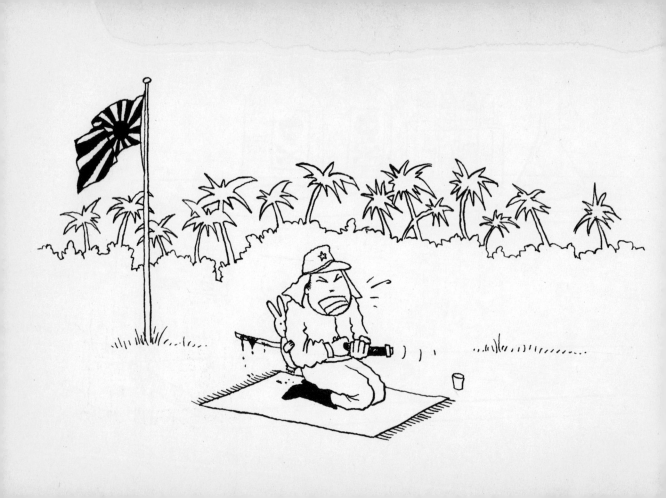

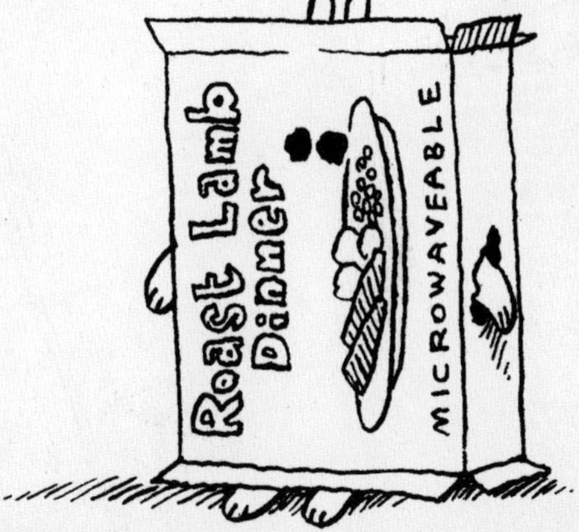
Roast Lamb Dinner
MICROWAVEABLE

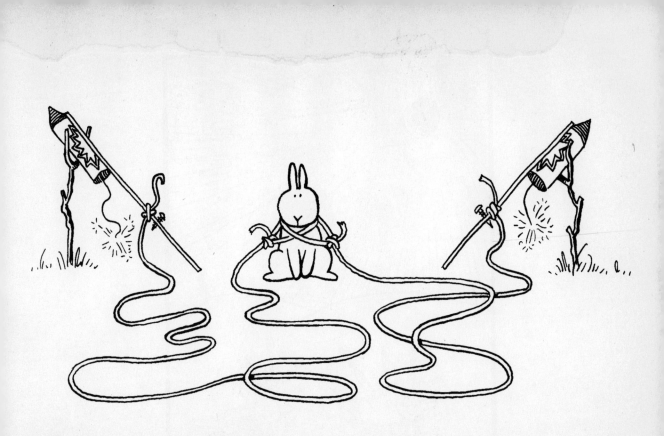

EPILOGUE

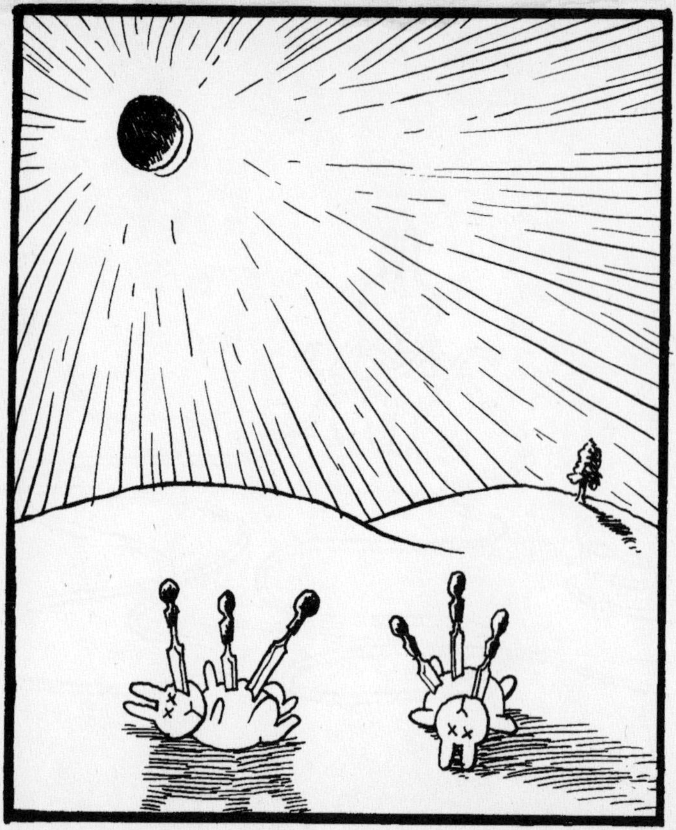

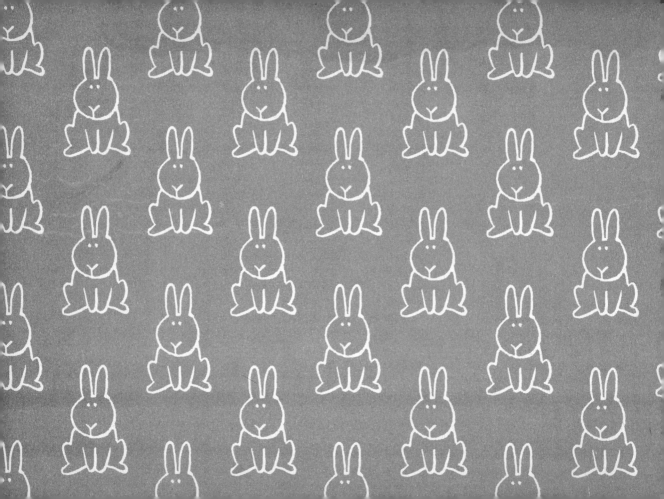